Challengers from the Sidelines

Understanding America's Violent Far-Right

THE COMBATING TERRORISM CENTER AT WEST POINT
www.ctc.usma.edu

November 2012

The views expressed in this report are the author's and do not necessarily reflect those of the Combating Terrorism Center, U.S. Military Academy, Department of Defense or U.S. government.

Introduction

In the last few years, and especially since 2007, there has been a dramatic rise in the number of attacks and violent plots originating from individuals and groups who self-identify with the far-right of American politics. These incidents cause many to wonder whether these are isolated attacks, an increasing trend, part of increasing societal violence, or attributable to some other condition. To date, however, there has been limited systematic documentation and analysis of incidents of American domestic violence.

This study provides a conceptual foundation for understanding different far-right groups and then presents the empirical analysis of violent incidents to identify those perpetrating attacks and their associated trends. Through a comprehensive look at the data, this study addresses three core questions:

(1) What are the main current characteristics of the violence produced by the far right?

(2) What type of far-right groups are more prone than others to engage in violence? How are characteristics of particular far-right groups correlated with their tendency to engage in violence?

(3) What are the social and political factors associated with the level of far-right violence? Are there political or social conditions that foster or discourage violence?

It is important to note that this study concentrates on those individuals and groups who have actually perpetuated violence and is not a comprehensive analysis of the political causes with which some far-right extremists identify. While the ability to hold and appropriately articulate diverse political views is an American strength, extremists committing acts of violence in the name of those causes undermine the freedoms that they purport to espouse.

The Landscape of the American Violent Far Right

There are three major ideological movements within the American violent far right: a racist/white supremacy movement, an anti-federalist movement and a fundamentalist movement. The ideological characteristics of the different movements affect their operations in terms of tactics used, targets selected, and operations conducted.

The racist movement is comprised of white supremacy groups such as the *KKK*, neo-Nazi groups such as the *National Alliance* and Skinheads groups such as the *Hammerskin Nation*. The groups comprising this movement are interested in preserving or restoring what they perceive as the appropriate and natural racial and cultural hierarchy, by enforcing social and political control over non-Aryans/nonwhites such as African Americans, Jews, and various immigrant communities. Therefore, their ideological foundations are based mainly on ideas of racism, segregation, xenophobia, and nativism (rejection of foreign norms and practices). In line with the movement's ideology, the great majority of attacks perpetrated by the racist groups are aimed against individuals or groups affiliated with a specific minority ethnic group, or identifiable facilities (mosques, synagogues, or schools affiliated with minority communities). However, while the KKK extremists are heavily involved in acts of vandalism, extremists from Skinheads and Neo-Nazi groups are more likely to engage in attacks against people, including mass casualty attacks.

Violence derived from the modern anti-federalist movement appeared in full force only in the early to mid-1990s and is interested in undermining the influence, legitimacy and effective sovereignty of the federal government and its proxy organizations. The anti-federalist rationale is multifaceted, and includes the beliefs that the American political system and its proxies were hijacked by external forces interested in promoting a "New World Order" (NWO) in which the United States will be absorbed into the United Nations or another version of global government. They also espouse strong convictions regarding the federal government, believing it to be corrupt and tyrannical, with a natural tendency to intrude on individuals' civil and constitutional rights. Finally, they support civil activism, individual freedoms, and self government. Extremists in the anti-federalist movement direct most their violence against the federal government and its proxies in law enforcement.

Lastly, the fundamentalist stream, which includes mainly Christian Identity groups such as the *Aryan Nations*, fuse religious fundamentalism with traditional white supremacy and racial tendencies, thus promoting ideas of nativism, exclusionism, and racial superiority through a unique interpretation of religious texts that focuses on division of humanity according to primordial attributes. More specifically, these groups maintain that a correct interpretation of the holy texts reveals that it is not the people of Israel but the Anglo-Saxons who are the chosen people and therefore assert their natural superior status. Moreover, the war between the forces of light and darkness, as portrayed in the Bible, will be (or has already been) manifested through a racial war between the white Anglo-Saxon nation and various non-Anglo-Saxon ethnic groups. Operationally, violence carried out by extremists associated with Identity groups focuses on minorities and Identity members have a higher tendency to engage in mass casualty attacks in comparison to other movements.

The typology illustrates that extremists link their behavior with their underlying ideology and reinforce each other in the organizational frameworks of the American violent far right. From a theoretical perspective, this constitutes a further indication of the perception among some parts of the academic community that terrorism is an instrument of symbolic discourse which is shared by violent groups and their adversaries. Target selection is thus not based just on operational considerations, but is one component, among others, that allows extremist groups to shape their message using violent practices. Timing, weapons used, and target locations are only part of all possible components that shape the symbolic message conveyed by any specific attack. In this context, the policy implications are clear. If the different far right extremist groups are driven by different ideological sentiments, and are thus also engaged in distinguishable tactics, then the counterterrorism response must be tailored appropriately for the movement involved.

Trends of Violence

This study also seeks to explain how both exogenous and endogenous factors may shape the characteristics of American far right violence, including political, demographic, and economic factors. Findings indicate that contentious and conservative political environments as well as the political empowerment are positively associated with the volume of violence; thus, it is not only feelings of deprivation that motivate those involved in far right violence, but also the sense of empowerment that emerges when the political system is perceived to be increasingly permissive to far right ideas. These trends contradict predominant perceptions which associate motivational forces that facilitate political violence with the unbalanced allocation of goods, and provide support for explanations which focus on correlations between violence and perceived changes in the sociopolitical structure.

While the findings are not particularly strong with regard to the relationship between the level of violence and economic factors, when looking at the trends in violence not only in relation to time, but also across space, and considering demographic indicators, it is clear that the violence is concentrated in heterogeneous areas, thus supporting theoretical assumptions associating intra-community violence with community cohesiveness and its members' perceptions regarding community boundaries. It is therefore clear from a policy perspective that more effort is needed to create effective integration mechanisms in areas in which we see growing ethnic, religious and cultural diversity.

Finally, the study provides additional insights that raise new questions for further research, such as the perceived limited correlation between the level of violence and the proportion and size of certain minority groups; changing trends in cooperation between various ideological streams; the shift of the violence from the South to other parts of the country; changes in the balance of power within the movements; and the clear decline of some of the groups, such as anti-abortionist extremists. This study is intended to represent a point of departure for further exploration of the American far right in addition to informing current research and policy discussions.

Table of Contents

Part 1- Conceptual Foundations and Historical Review   **8**

  1. Introduction   9

  2. Conceptualizing the Far Right   13

  3. Conceptualizing the American Far Right   19

Part 2 – Empirical and Theoretical Foundations: Explaining American Far-Right Violence   **84**

  4. Empirical Picture: General overview of the American Violent Far Right   85

  5. Empirical Picture: The Perpetrators and Trends among Specific Movements   120

  6. Concluding Remarks   146

Part 1 – Conceptual Foundations and Historical Review

This operation took some long-term planning and, throughout the entire time, these soldiers were aware that their lives would be sacrificed for their cause. If an Aryan wants an example of 'Victory or Valhalla', look no further (Thomas Metzger, *Leader of the White Aryan Resistance,* in response to 9/11 attacks)[1]

…We should be blowing up NYC and DC, not waiting for a bunch of camel Jockeys to do it for us (Victor Gerhard, *Vanguard News Network*)[2]

---

[1] Martin Durham, *White Rage: The Extreme Right and American Politics* (New York: Routledge, 2007), 112.
[2] Victor Gerhard, "Payback's A Bitch," *Vanguard News Network,* http://www.vanguardnewsnetwork.com/v1/index117.htm (accessed 24 May 2012).

1. Introduction

Oklahoma state trooper Charles J. Hanger was patrolling interstate highway I-35 in the morning hours of 19 April 1995 when he suddenly observed an old yellow Mercury Marquis with no license plates.[3] After signaling the driver to park the car on the sideway, Hanger approached the car, and his suspicions were instantly raised. Not only were the plates missing, but the driver also reacted in an unusual manner. Instead of waiting within the car as most people would do, he stepped out and started calmly engaging the state trooper in conversation, admitting he had neither insurance nor license plates. The driver also admitted that he had a knife and a loaded handgun in his possession, the latter without an appropriate license. In the state of Oklahoma, these infractions result in immediate detention. To complete the unusual picture, the driver was wearing a shirt printed with provocative phrases. The front of the shirt quoted the words shouted by John Wilkes Booth after shooting Abraham Lincoln: "Thus, always, to tyrants," and on the back was Thomas Jefferson's statement: "The tree of liberty must be refreshed from time to time with the blood of patriots and tyrants."[4] As expected, the driver, Timothy James McVeigh, was arrested and taken to the Perry District Detention Center to await trial for illegal possession of a firearm. However, three days later, the FBI concluded that this was the least of his crimes. Apparently, McVeigh was responsible for the most devastating terrorist attack on US soil until then.

Little more than an hour before he had been arrested, McVeigh had driven a Ryder truck loaded with over 6500 pounds of explosives and parked it near the Alfred P. Murrah Federal building in Oklahoma City. The subsequent explosion, two minutes after 9am, had almost completely destroyed the northeast side of the building, although failing to raze the building as McVeigh had hoped. One hundred and sixty-eight people, including 19 children, were killed. Hundreds were injured. The city of Oklahoma, and large parts of the country, were in a state of shock and disbelief.[5]

---

[3] Michel Lue and Dan Herbeck, *American Terrorist* (New York: Regan Books–HarperCollins, 2002), 239–40.

[4] Ibid., 240–46.

[5] For more details on the attack see Andrew Gumbel and Roger G. Charles, *Oklahoma City: What the Investigation Missed and Why it Still Matters* (New York: William Morrow, 2012); Lue and Herbeck, 223–32; Emily M. Bernstein, "Terror in Oklahoma: The overview; evidence linking suspect to blast offered in court," *NY Times*, 28 April, 1995, http://www.nytimes.com/1995/04/28/us/terror-oklahoma-overview-evidence-linking-suspect-blast-offered-court.html?ref=timothyjamesmcveigh (accessed 2 November 2012); Robert D. McFadden, "Terror in Oklahoma: John Doe No. 1 -- A special report.; A Life of Solitude

The FBI investigation revealed that the attack was not the act of a single fanatic, but an operation planned by a small network consisting of four people,[6] all with ties to the American far-right subculture.[7] Motivated by their rage, frustration and resentment towards the federal government, they decided to take matters into their own hands. For them, the only way to raise the awareness of the American public of what they perceived as the growing corruption and incompetence of the federal government, as well as its increasing tendency to violate civil and constitutional rights, was by conducting a dramatic mass-casualty attack, killing as many representatives of the Federal government as possible.[8]

Although unique in its impact and in the level of destruction it caused, the case of McVeigh's network is not exceptional in terms of the social, political, economic, and contextual conditions that fostered its members' radicalization. As in many other violent political groups, the background and the radicalization process of the network's members appear to be associated with a supportive social enclave, sentiments of alienation from the mainstream culture and political system, personal financial and mental crises, and previous experience with exercising extreme violence.[9] Hence, evidence suggests that the use of theory deriving from the political violence and terrorism literature is valuable in deciphering violent manifestations of the American

---

and Obsessions," *NY Times*, 4 May, 1995, http://www.nytimes.com/1995/05/04/us/terror-oklahoma-john-doe-no-1-special-report-life-solitude-obsessions.html?ref=timothyjamesmcveigh (accessed 2 November 2012); Joe Swickard, "The Life of Terry Nichols,"
Detroit Free Press: Seattle Times News Services, 11 May, 1995, http://www.webcitation.org/5wovr8qZG (accessed 2 November 2012); "After Action Report: Alfred P. Murrah Federal Building Bombing," (The Oklahoma Department of Civil Emergency Management: archived 25 August, 2003), available per request from the Author/CTC.
[6] McVeigh's trial proceedings suggest that as many as six people were involved in the operation on some level, including Terry Nichols and Michael and Lori Fortier; in other words, it was not a "lone-wolf" operation. See - http://law2.umkc.edu/faculty/projects/ftrials/mcveigh/mcveightranscript.html, for more details.
[7] For detailed discussion on how far right ideology is being defined and conceptualized see chapter two of this study; see also John Kifner, "Oklahoma Blast: A Tale in 2 Books?" (NY Times: 21 August 1995), http://www.nytimes.com/1995/08/21/us/oklahoma-blast-a-tale-in-2-books.html?ref=timothyjamesmcveigh (accessed 2 November 2012). It was also found that McVeigh's network was associated with the Aryan Republican Army (ARA), a white supremacy group that waged a shadow war against the federal government through the mid-1990s, striking at least 22 banks across the Midwest in an attempt to finance an all-out race war, see Max McCoy, "Timothy McVeigh and the Neo-Nazi Bankrobbers," (Fortean Times: November 2004), http://www.webcitation.org/5woxP0H7c (accessed 2 November 2012).
[8] Lue and Herbeck, 117–58.
[9] Ibid.

far-right.[10] However, does the scale of the phenomenon justify a closer and more rigorous examination? Or are we dealing with a marginal phenomenon? Looking at recent trends of far-right violence in the United States could facilitate the formulation of an answer.

Until the attack in Oklahoma, very few people noticed that the previous years (1994–5) had been characterized by a striking rise in the number of violent attacks by American far-right groups. After a relatively quiet 1993 in which the American far-right was almost non-active (only nine attacks), no less than 75 attacks were perpetrated in the following year, with another 30 attacks in the first three months of 1995.[11] What occurred in Oklahoma was not a random, isolated attack but part of a wave of far-right violence which was fueled by specific political and social conditions. Although following "OKBOMB,"[12] the US government significantly augmented the resources and measures employed to detect and dismantle violent and potentially dangerous far-right associations, far-right groups did not cease to exist. Some of them adapted to the growing governmental scrutiny by shifting to milder, less militant activities; others formed new organizational entities in place of the old ones, hoping to deter suspicion. Combined with the emergence of the Jihadi threat, this facilitated a prevailing sense that the far right was in decline. However, this apparent interlude is over. In the last few years, especially since 2007, there has been a dramatic rise in the number of attacks and violent plots originating in the far-right of American politics. Does this reflect the return of far-right violence? And if so, should we expect, as in previous waves, the emergence of groups which will be willing to initiate mass casualty attacks, similar to the one perpetrated by McVeigh and his associates? The current study will assess the current and future threat from the far right by providing answers to three core questions:

---

[10] It should be noted that domestic political violence in the US is not restricted to the right side of the political spectrum, although it seems that recent left wing terrorism is more related to Environmental Animal Rights policies (see groups such as ELF and ALF), Paul Joosse, "Leaderless Resistance and Ideological Inclusion: The Case of the Earth Liberation Front," *Terrorism and Political Violence*, 19(3) (2007), 351–68; Stefan H. Leader and Peter Probst, "The Earth Liberation Front and Environmental Terrorism," *Terrorism and Political Violence*, 15(4) (2003), 37–8.

[11] The data is based on the CTC's Far-Right violence dataset. Detailed description of the dataset is provided at part two of this study.

[12] The name given to the federal investigation following the attack: see Richard A. Serano, *One of Ours: Timothy McVeigh and the Oklahoma City Bombing*. (New York: W. W. Norton & Company, 1998), 139–41.

1) What are the main current characteristics of the violence produced by the far right?

2) What type of far-right groups are more prone than others to become involved in violence? How are the characteristics of those particular far-right groups correlated with their tendency to engage in violence?

3) What are the social and political factors associated with the level of far-right violence? Are there political or social conditions that foster or discourage violence?

The first part of the study provides a contextual foundation by conceptualizing the American far right and then depicting its ideological and organizational/operational development. The second part analyzes the violence and radicalization processes in the different streams of the violent American far right using a comprehensive dataset that documents American far-right violence in the last 22 years.[13] The last part of the study is an assessment of the future trajectory of American far right violence.

---

[13] The primary resources are used extensively in the first part of the study, with quantitative data used prevailingly in the second part.

2. Conceptualizing the Far Right

2.1 - Conceptual Chaos

The study of far-right movements and parties has for years suffered from terminological chaos and the absence of a clear and conceptual framework. Hence, it is not merely that different scholars have used different terms to describe these political groups, such as far right,[14] extreme right,[15] right wing populism,[16] and radical right,[17] but that there are also disagreements regarding the kind of ideological foundations that constitute the far-right paradigm.[18] Moreover, the particularities of different political systems also facilitate confusion. For example, in the case of Israel, far right designation is strongly linked to views which justify extreme means for preserving Israel's control over the West Bank and Gaza Strip, and the promotion of the idea of "the Greater Land of Israel."[19] In both Israel and the United States the far right encompasses strong religious dimensions, since in both countries religious ideology and fundamentalist interpretation of holy texts are frequently suborned as justification for far right extremism. However, in Europe it appears that the role of religion is more marginal, and immigration and integration policies are the hallmark of far-right rhetoric.[20] Although in the European and Israeli arenas we find a relatively cohesive far-right universe in terms of its historical origins, ideological tenets and organizational manifestations, including presence within the legitimate political system, in the American case we can identify greater ideological and organizational diversity coupled with a more marginal presence in political institutions.

---

[14] Jonathan Marcus, "Exorcising Europe's Demons: a Far Right Resurgence?" *The Washington Quarterly*, 23(4) (2000), 31–40; Angus Roxburgh, *Preachers of Hate: The Rise of the Far Right* (London: Gibson Square, 2002).

[15] Paul Hainsworth, "Introduction to the Extreme Right," in Paul Hainsworth ed. *The Politics of the Extreme Right: From The Margins to the Mainstream* (London: Pinter, 2000) 1–17.

[16] Hans-Georg Betz, *Radical Right-Wing Populism in Western Europe* (New York: Palgrave Macmillan, 1994).

[17] Sabrina Ramet, "Defining the Radical Right: Values and Behaviors of Organized Intolerance in Post Communist Central and Eastern Europe,"in Sabrina Ramet ed. *Radical Right in Central and Eastern Europe since 1989* (University Park: Pennsylvania State University Press, 1999) 3–27; Pedahzur Ami and Brichta Avarham, "The Institutionalization of Extreme Right Wing Charismatic Parties: A Paradox?" *Party Politics* 8(1) (2002), 31–49.

[18] Cass Mudde, *Populist Radical Right Parties* (Cambridge: Cambridge University Press, 2007), 11–14.

[19] See e.g., Ehud Sprinzak, *The Ascendance of Israel's Radical Right* (Oxford: Oxford University Press, 1991).

[20] See e.g., Danny Rubinstein, *Gush Emunim* (Tel Aviv: Hkibutz Hameuchad, 1982); Ehud Sprinzak, *Fundamentalism, Terrorism, and Democracy: The Case of the Gush Emunim Underground* (Washington D.C.: Smithsonian Institution, 1987).

Similar to the attempts of terrorism scholars to confront the absence of an agreed definition of terrorism, two complementing conceptual approaches have evolved to describe the far right. The first approach aims at a minimal definition based on the "lowest common denominator" principle, looking for the maximum number of elements that have characterized all manifestations of far-right political activism. The second approach attempts to achieve an inclusive definition based on the "most similar system design," seeking the greatest number of possible similarities among at least some parts of the research population.[21] In essence, the second approach has reflected an effort to expand the boundaries of the far-right "family" and decrease the extent of gray areas between the mainstream right and the far right. While most of the abovementioned literature was written in the context of far-right parties, and not violent groups per se, this body of literature is still useful for constructing the ideological boundaries of the current study research population. Hence, the following paragraphs briefly portray the basic and expanded conceptual frameworks of far-right ideology. This will be followed by adaptation of these conceptual frameworks to the case of the American far-right and the formulation of a typology of American far-right groups.

2.2 - The Ideology of the Far Right

Before conceptualizing far-right ideology, it is important to note that the following paragraphs, while using concepts which may be perceived as pejorative, are not intended to provide moral judgment of the groups which comprise the far right, but to point out their shared ideas and norms by using concepts which are accepted and well defined within the academic literature. These norms and ideas will be further exemplified and brought to life in later parts of this study, which will provide high-resolution analysis of the ideology of the violent American far right.

If there is one ideological doctrine about which there is almost full consensus regarding its importance for understanding the far-right worldview, it is that of nationalism. Historically, the literature on nationalism has taken diverse directions and is extremely rich, but in its varying guises it usually refers to the association between ethnic, cultural

---

[21] For further debate on the two approaches see Mudde (2007), 13–15.

and/or linguistic identity and political expression, or more simply put, the convergence of a cultural framework with a political entity.[22]

In the context of the far-right worldview, nationalism takes an extreme form of full convergence between one polity or territory and one ethnic or national collective.[23] Two elements are required for the fulfillment of this version of the nationalist doctrine. The first is that of *internal homogenization*, i.e., the aspiration that all residents or citizens of the polity will share the same national origin and ethnic characteristics.[24] The second is the element of *external exclusiveness*, the aspiration that all individuals belonging to a specific national or ethnic group will reside in the homeland.[25] As will be demonstrated later, in the context of the American far-right the tendency is to emphasize the first element. Several explanations can be provided for that inclination. First, in the context of liberal democracies the limited control on the movement of population departing the country in comparison with the greater capacity to control incoming population makes policies promoting internal homogenization more attainable than those dealing with external exclusiveness. Second, since the homeland is perhaps the most essential element in ensuring the ongoing existence of the nation, there is more emphasis on protecting the ethnic homogeneity of the population residing in the homeland than on the need to consolidate the entire collective within one territory. Finally, the various dimensions and implications of internal homogenization make it attractive to far-right groups in terms of political mobilization.[26] In simple terms, people tend to care more about the homogeneity of their surroundings than the need to reduce the size of their nation's Diaspora.

---

[22] Ernest Gellner, *Nation and Nationalism* (Oxford: Basil Blakwell, 1983); E. J. Hobsbawm, *Nations and Nationalism since 1780: Programme, Myth, Reality* (Cambridge: Cambridge University Press, 1990); For works which provide a relevant overview of literature on Nationalism, see Anthony D. Smith, *Nationalism and Modernism: A Critical Survey of Recent Theories of Nations and Nationalism* (London: Routledge, 1998); Walker Connor, *Ethnonationalism: The Quest for Understanding* (Princeton: Princeton University Press, 1994); Daniele Conversi, "Reassessing Theories of Nationalism: Nationalism as Boundary Maintenance and Creation," *Nationalism and Ethnic Politics*, 1(1) (1995), 73–85; and Umut Ozkirimli, *Theories of Nationalism: A Critical Overview* (Basingstoke: Macmillan, 2000).

[23] See further discussion, see Betz (1994).

[24] Koen Koch, "Back to Sarajevo or Beyond Trianon? Some Thoughts on the Problem of Nationalism in Eastern Europe," *Netherlands Journal of Social Sciences* 27(1) (1991), 29–42.

[25] Ibid.; Mudde, *Ideology of the Extreme Right* (Manchester: Manchester University Press, 2000), 169.

[26] Pedahzur and Perliger illustrate this in their analysis of the Israeli Far-Right, see Ami Pedahzur and Arie Perliger, "An Alternative Approach for Defining the Boundaries of 'Party Families': Examples from the Israeli Extreme Right-Wing Party Scene," *Australian Journal of Political Science,* 39(2) (2004), 285–305.

The idea of nativism represents a wider implementation of the internal homogenization concept. Internal homogenization rejects the incorporation and recognition of those embodying different ethnic and national traits as part of the nation. In addition, nativism adds opposition to external influence, whether on a cultural, religious, or normative basis. Foreign influence is perceived as a threat to the entirety and homogeneity of the nation and, as a result, to its resiliency, its ability to counter external threats and to preserve its essential traits.[27] The concept of nativism explains why in many cases the activities of far-right groups do not only oppose foreigners, but also those citizens who promote what is perceived as non-native norms, practices or values. By extending the idea of internal homogenization as it is reflected in the concept of nativism, proponents of far-right ideology establish comfortable ground—and a moral justification—for actions against the nation's enemies from within.[28]

While ideas corresponding to internal homogenization and nativism are to be found in all far-right groups, thereby constituting a minimal definition of far-right ideology, there are other ideological elements which are considered almost consensual, and are present in the majority of far-right groups or parties, although not in all of them, and not always as core principles. These can be divided into two groups. The first includes concepts that complement the rationale of internal homogenization through xenophobia, racism and exclusionism. Xenophobia involves behaviors and sentiments derived from fear, hate and hostility towards groups which are perceived as alien or strange, including people with alternative sexual preferences, styles of living and behavior;[29] racism refers to the same sentiments, but based on racial grounds, such as belief in the national and moral significance of natural and hereditary differences between races, and the conviction that certain races are superior to others.[30] Finally,

---

[27] John Higham, *Strangers in the Land: Patterns of American Nativism, 1860-1925* (New Brunswick: Rutgers University Press, 1955); Mudde (2007), 18; Niambi M. Carter and Efren O. Perez, "If it's White, is it Right? National Attachments, African Americans, and Hostility to Immigrants." Paper presented at the American Political Science Association Annual Meeting, Boston, MA (2008).

[28] Mudde (2007), 19.

[29] Hainsworth (2000), 11; Mudde, "Right-wing Extremism Analyzed: a Comparative Analysis of the Ideologies of Three Alleged Right-Wing Extremist Parties (NPD, NDP. CP'86)," *European Journal of Political Research*, 27 (1995), 203–24.

[30] Robert Miles and Annie Phizacklea, "Some Introductory Observations on Race and Politics in Britain," in ed. Robert Mies and Annie Phizacklea, *Racism and Political Action in Britain* (London: Routledge & Kegan Paul, 1979), 1–27; on different approaches for the conceptualization of racism see Kevin Reilly; Stephen Kaufman; Angela Bodino, *Racism: a global reader* (Armonk, N.Y: M.E. Sharpe, 2003).

exclusionism is the practical manifestation of these sentiments on the communal or state level. Practically, outsiders are excluded from specific spheres of the social, economic and political arena, such as the labor market, the educational system and residential areas.[31]

However, the intellectual property of the far right is not limited to defining the boundaries between insiders and outsiders, but also strives to shape the political culture and relations between the political system and society. These elements, which constitute the second group as almost consensual, include an enduring affinity towards traditional values, what is referred to as a "strong state," and anti-democratic sentiment.

Regarding affinity towards traditional values, a common perception is that liberal/left-wing and conservative worldviews are different in their time orientation. While liberal worldviews are future- or progressive -oriented, conservative perspectives are more past-oriented, and in general, are interested in preserving the status quo.[32] The far right represents a more extreme version of conservatism, as its political vision is usually justified by the aspiration to restore or preserve values and practices that are part of the idealized historical heritage of the nation or ethnic community.[33] In many cases these past-oriented perspectives help to formulate a nostalgic and romantic ideological aura which makes these groups attractive for many who aspire to restore the halcyon days of a clear hierarchy of values and norms.[34] While traditional values provide an important distinction between the far right and other political streams, it should be noted that it does not typify the ideology of all extremist organizations; Closer inspection reveals that specific parts of the new waves of far-right groups, especially those occurring since the 1980s, do not always adhere to traditional values or tend to emphasize them.[35]

As part of the nostalgic sentiments promoted by far-right groups, there is an emphasis on the clear and natural order that is regarded by its proponents as characterizing the idealized past. Hence many of these groups advance policies related to strengthening

---

[31] Pedahzur and Perliger (2004).

[32] An effective summary of current and traditional perspectives regarding the nature of conservatism (in comparison to liberal ideological frameworks) can be found in Vincent Andrew, *Modern Political Ideologies* (Oxford, UK and Cambridge, USA: Blackwell, 1995), 55–8.

[33] Hans-Georg Betz, "Politics of Resentment: Right-wing Radicalism in West Germany," *Comparative Politics*, 23 (1990), 15–60.

[34] Hainsworth (2000), 12.

[35] This will be exemplified later in the ideological analysis of the far-right groups.

state authorities (the "strong state" position) and "law and order," as part of their attempts to restore past glory and prevent further societal deterioration.[36] Far-right parties in Europe, for example, have traditionally demanded more resources for law enforcement, and for releasing the judicial system from the liberal constraints preventing the delivery of appropriate, usually harsher verdicts.[37] In the American case, this tendency is reflected in classic vigilantism, i.e., activities aimed at assisting governmental authorities in "restoring order to society."[38]

Finally, many recognize antidemocratic dispositions among various far-right groups.[39] There are conceptual and practical dimensions to this tendency. On the conceptual level, there are irreconcilable tensions between core nationalist elements, internal homogenization and nativism of far right groups, on the one hand, and the liberal-democratic value system, on the other hand. Such tensions tend to push far-right groups to adopt an "anti-system" stance and revisionist views of the democratic system. These tensions translate on the practical level: while far-right groups' ideology is designed to exclude minorities and foreigners, the liberal-democratic system is designed to emphasize civil rights, minority rights and the balance of power.

To conclude, historically the far-right literature has provided numerous definitions and conceptual and analytical frameworks for understanding the ideological paradigm of these groups. As indicated by Mudde, by the mid-1990s no less than 28 different definitions were introduced, including close to 60 different elements.[40] However, it seems that in the last few years there has been growing consensus regarding the importance and the central role of the concepts discussed above in far-right ideology, and for the need to establish core definitional elements such as these. The above elements will be used in this study to sketch the boundaries of the American far-right. Ideological components which have been excluded from the above discussion are those which overlap with more specialized ideological concepts e.g., anti-parliamentarianism, or which are less ideological per se and refer more to the practice of mobilization, such as populism, or to the internal structure and organizational culture of far-right groups, e.g., authoritarianism.

---

[36] Mudde (1995), 216–17; see also discussion at Mudde (2007), 21–2.
[37] Ibid.
[38] For further discussion on the different types of vigilantism, see Ami Pedahzur and Arie Perliger, "The Causes of Vigilant Political Violence: The Case of Jewish Settlers," *Civil Wars*, 6(3) (2003), 9–30.
[39] Ibid, 214–15; Pedahzur and Perliger (2004).
[40] Mudde (2007), 11–13.

3. Conceptualizing the American Far Right

In order to understand the dynamics and the impact of racism, we must view it as a faith—and, for the American society, a permanent belief system rather than a transient apparition. Its longevity has been tried and tested. It now occupies a place in the American value pantheon alongside such concepts as democracy and liberty, though one would ordinarily view this combination as contradictory.

Rutledge M. Dennis "Socialization and Racism"[41]

The American far-right was for many years associated with the militant activism of the *Ku Klux Klan* (KKK). While the KKK and its modern white supremacist offspring are still active, in recent decades other types of ideological groups have begun to populate the American far-right universe. Among these are militias, Christian Identity groups, Skinheads and neo-Nazis. From an analytical point of view, this development has had two major implications. First, the far right has become more vibrant and more ideologically and structurally diverse than ever before. Second, the boundaries of the far right have grown less distinct as many of the new groups have occasionally become inspired by ideas and practices which originated from outside conventional far-right discourse. Both these implications reflect the need to develop an effective typology in order to portray a more accurate and nuanced picture of the American far-right, as well as for understanding its ideological development. A useful analytical instrument for the construction of such a typology is the standard classification proposed originally by McCarthy and Zald[42] which differentiates between Social Movement (SM), Social Movement Organization (SMO) and Social Movement Industry (SMI). The first element is defined as a set of opinions and beliefs of a segment of the population, and represents preferences for changing some aspects of social or political construction; the second, SMO, is the formal organizational manifestation of the social movement. The Social Movement Industry is a collection of SMOs that have as their goal the attainment of the broadest preferences of a social movement.

---

[41] Rutledge M. Dennis, "Socialization and Racism: The White Experience," in ed. Benjamin P. Bowser and Raymond G. Hunt *Impacts of Racism on White Americans* (Thousand Oaks, California: Sage Publications, 1981).

[42] D. John McCarty and N. Mayer Zald, "Resource Mobilization and Social Movements: A Partial Theory," American Journal of Sociology, 82(6) (1977), 1212–41.

As will be explained in the following sections, in the case of the American far right we were able to identify three separate SMIs, each comprising various SMOs that represent the ideological tenets of a distinct social movement (see Figure 1). This was done by applying a domestic group dataset constructed specifically for the current study and which documents different characteristics of all American far-right groups that have been involved in violent activities. Based on the dataset, two levels of analysis have been used to distinguish between different types of far-right groups: (a) ideological analysis; (b) organizational and operational analysis. The following two sections will investigate the different ideological frameworks which constitute the three SMs, and the organizational and operational patterns of the respective SMOs and SMIs.

3.1 - The Ideological Universe of the American Far Right, 1865–2000s

Ideologies are dynamic and fairly coherent sets of symbols, concepts and values which provide a framework for organizing and determining different dimensions of human activities and interactions, social institutions, and the way new events and political, social and cultural developments are interpreted.[43] The dynamic nature of ideologies is conspicuous in the history of the American far-right, as ideas, concepts, and values have consistently been re-shaped, integrated with one another and re-evaluated. In order to identify the main ideological concepts populating the American far-right, the ideological platform of each group in the group dataset has been analyzed, and each of the ideological components identified has been graded on a scale based on its prominence in the group's ideological platform according to the following categories: 1) non-appearance; 2) indication; 3) present; and 4) core.[44] Based on this analysis, as already mentioned above, three main schools of thought have been identified, each representing a distinct social movement.

---

[43] For comprehensive discussion on the definition of ideology (including in historical context) see Kathleen Knight, "Transformations of the Concept of Ideology in the Twentieth Century," *American Political Science Review*, 100(4) (2006), 619–26; Malcolm B. Hamilton, "The Elements of the Concept of Ideology," *Political Studies*, 35(1) (2006), 18–38.

[44] "Non-appearance" means that the ideological components are absent from the group's ideological platform or terminology; "indication" means that the ideological components are implied or mentioned briefly, but definitely are not emphasized or part of the group's core ideological tenets; "present" indicates that the ideological components are being mentioned frequently and used to support the group's core ideological principles. Finally, "core" indicates that the ideological components are part of the basic raison d'être of the group.

3.1.1 - Racist/White Supremacy Movement: Ideological Foundations

The groups comprising the racist movement are interested in preserving or restoring what they perceive as the natural racial and cultural hierarchy by enforcing social and political control over non-Aryans[45]/nonwhites, such as African Americans, Jews and the members of various immigrant communities. Their ideological foundations are based mainly on ideas of nativism, internal homogeneity, racism, exclusionism and xenophobia. Although other popular components of far-right ideology—a strong affinity for law and order; traditional values; and anti-democratic dispositions—are exhibited by some of these groups, they are clearly secondary.

The birth of the racist movement is usually associated with the emergence of the original KKK in Tennessee in 1865. At its peak this association included half a million members.[46] Although in the aftermath of the Civil War it quickly declined and was officially disbanded in 1869, it still provided the ideological foundation for the white supremacy paradigm as exemplified in the declared goal of the first KKK convention (1867) in Nashville: "To maintain the supremacy of the White race in the republic,"[47] and similarly in the words of the KKK historian William Pierce Randel in describing the motivation of the first KKK founders: "America was founded by the White race and for the white race…any effort to transfer control to the black race was an obvious violation of the constitution…."[48] At that time, the main effort of the KKK in this regard was to thwart attempts to impose changes to the social, economic and political order and culture in the Southern states, and especially to maintain the asymmetric relations between the white majority and African Americans.[49] As explained by Horn, "The Klan was doing only what the regional majority wanted—preserving the American way of life as white Southerners defined it."[50] This was done by targeting "carpetbaggers

---

[45] The term Aryan today usually refers to Anglo-Saxon Protestants, whose ethnic origin is from the central and northern regions of Europe.

[46] Michael Newton and Judy Ann Newton, *Ku Klux Klan: An Encyclopedia* (New York: Garland Publication, 1991).

[47] A Betty Dobratz and Stephanie Shanks-Meile, *"White Power, White Pride!" The White Separatist Movement in the Unites States* (New York: Twayne Publishers, 1997), 36.

[48] Chester Quarles, *Ku Klux Klan and related American Racialist and Antisemitic Organizations : a History and Analysis* (Jefferson, N.C.: McFarland, 1999), 40.

[49] Ibid., 37.

[50] Stanley Fitzgerald Horn, *Invisible Empire; The Story of the Ku Klux Klan, 1866-1871* (Boston: Houghton Mifflin Co., 1939), 3–4.

[northern entrepreneurs], scalawags, and upwardly mobile Negros in a terroristic way."[51]

The early decades of the twentieth century witnessed the rise to prominence of far-right ideologies in Central and Eastern Europe. Similar trends, on a smaller scale, were to be found in the United States as well with the re-establishment of the KKK (the "Second Klan") by "Colonel" William Simmons in 1915, and the appearance of the American version of National Socialism in the early 1930s. As for the KKK, Simmons and his associates' success in creating a relatively romantic, non-violent and anti-corporatist image for the new KKK, facilitated the mobilization of significant support not just from the traditional blue collar classes in the South, but also from no small segment of the middle and upper classes of urban Protestants.[52] Nonetheless, despite the mass nature the KKK assumed in the late 1920s, it is still important to note that the Klan leadership and the overall organizational ideology remained loyal to its original ideas of internal homogeneity, nativism and traditional ethics, which were reflected by its white supremacist, racist, anti-Semitic, anti-immigrant and anti-Catholic rhetoric. The "Klan Line" publication beginning in 1923 illustrates this: "The Anglo-Saxon is the type man of History. To him must yield the self-centered Hebrew, the cultured Greek, the virile Roman and Mystic Oriental...The KKK desires that its ruling members shall be of this all-conquering blood...the KKK was planned for the White Americans..."[53]

During the mid-1930s, the KKK was joined on the white supremacy scene by the *German-American Bund*, which was perhaps the predominant reflection of the growing sympathy among some German-Americans for National Socialism and its racist tendencies. In its 1938 convention, for example, the organization advocated a white, gentile-ruled US, gentile-controlled unions, and cleansing of the Hollywood film

---

[51] Quarles (1999), 31.

[52] Rory McVeigh, *Rise of the Ku Klux Klan* (Minneapolis: University of Minnesota, 2009), chapter 1; Dobratz and Shanks-Meile, 39; Arnold Rice, *Ku Klux Klan in American Politics* (New York: Haskell House Publishers LTD, 1972) 8; for other estimates regarding the size of the KKK at that time see also John Zerzan, "Rank and File Radicalism within the Ku Klux Klan," *Anarchy: Journal of Desire Armed*, (Summer 1993), 48–53; Robert Goldberg, *Hooded Empire: The Ku Klux Klan in Colorado* (Urbana: University of Illinois Press, 1981), viii.

[53] An unambiguous illustration of the strong racist foundation of the movement was provided by Simmons himself in a speech he delivered in Dallas in 1923, when he argued regarding African Americans that "They Have not, they cannot, attain the Anglo-Saxon level...the low mentality of savage ancestors, of Jungle environment, is inherent in the blood stream of the colored race..." see Rice, 20.

industry of all alien, subversive doctrines.[54] Hence, the *Bund* imported not just the nativist and racist ideology of Nazism, but also the perception that the nation was being manipulated and controlled by aliens and needed to be purified.[55] The concept of the hijacked government would be one of the ideological pillars of the militia movement which would emerge 60 years later.

The Second World War did not result in the eradication of American National Socialism. The dispersion of intense anti-German and anti-fascist sentiments among the American population prevented expansion or effective mobilization by neo-Nazi groups immediately after World War II. Nevertheless, since the late 1950s, and especially in the 1970s, there has been a reemergence of neo-Nazi ideology with the growth of groups such as the *American Nazi Party (ANP)*[56], the *Nationalist Socialist Party of America (NSPA)*, and the *National Alliance (NA)*, which, since the 1990s, has become the largest and most influential neo-Nazi group in the United States.[57] These groups did not merely adopt Nazi heritage, symbols, rituals and ideological foundations to justify and promote anti-Semitic, racist and nativist ideas, but also, endorsed full exclusionism, in line with the National Socialist tradition. More specifically, since they believed that territorial and racial purity was a condition for the survival of the white race, they developed the idea of enforced segregation, including programs to eliminate inferior races, i.e., Jews,[58] to expel others, i.e., African Americans,[59] or to divide the union into racially homogeneous geographical areas.[60]

Ideas of geographical segregation were also gradually adopted by different KKK branches in the late 1970s and early 1980s. These normally envisioned the creation of a white national government (or confederacy), which would facilitate cooperation

---

[54] Susan Canedy, *America's Nazis: A Democratic Dilemma* (Menlo Park, CA: Markgraf Publication Group, 1990), 191–2.

[55] See also Joachim Remak, "Friends of the New Germany: the Bund and German-American Relations," *Journal of American History* 29 (1) (1957), 38–41; Sander Diamond, *Nazi Movement in the United States: 1924–1941* (Ithaca: Cornell University, 1974).

[56] Which was later named the *National Socialist White People's Party (NSWPP)*.

[57] Southern Poverty Law Center report, "National Alliance: North America Largest Neo Nazi Group Flourishing," *Klanwatch Intelligence Report*, 82: 5-8 (1996); SOUTHERN POVERTY LAW CENTER report, "Active Hate Groups," *Klanwatch Intelligence Report*, 85: 19-22 (1997).

[58] H. William Schmaltz, *Hate: George Lincoln Rockwell and the American Nazi Party* (Washington: Brassey's, 1999), 2, 49–50, 100–101, 134; FBI file on ANP, 17.

[59] FBI file on ANP, pg. 17.

[60] Ibid.

between the "White States" in the face of the threats presented by other races. In 1984, for example, David Duke, who in the mid-1970s became one of the prominent figures in the KKK leadership, published a detailed program for concentrating different minorities in regional ghettos, while 80% of the country would be reserved for "pure," "white" Christian states.[61]

Duke was a strong advocate for mainstreaming the Klan's ideology and practices in order to move the organization from the "cow pastures" to the "hotel meeting rooms."[62] This plan involved the inclusion of Catholics in the organization, up-scaling the organization's propaganda to attract a more educated audience, especially students, as well as introducing policies for the induction of women into the organization.[63] Eventually, to facilitate his vision of a more socially and nationally acceptable white supremacy organization, he left the Klan and founded the *National Association for the Advancement of the White People (NAAWP)*.[64] For the framework of the new organization Duke adopted the rhetorical practices of the Civil Rights Movement. He framed his nativist ideas defensively, usually presenting himself as a leader of the movement for the promotion and protection of the rights of white people interested in preserving their heritage and culture.[65] This is not unexpected, as the sociological literature acknowledged that movements and counter-movements—i.e. The White supremacy and civil right movements—react and adapt to each other's actions, in what Zald and Useem describe as "a sometimes loosely coupled tango of mobilization and demobilization."[66]

This less militant framing of the classic KKK nativist and segregationist ideas contributed to Duke's popularity and convinced him to engage in mainstream politics. However, he was never able to translate his extremist popularity into significant

---

[61] James Ridgeway, *Blood in the Face: The Ku Klux Klan, Aryan Nations, Nazi Skinheads, and the Rise of a New White Culture* (London: Thunder's Mouth Press, 1995), 150–51.

[62] Wyn Craig Wade, *Fiery Cross: The Ku Klux Klan in America* (New York: Simon and Schuster, 1987), 368.

[63] ADL report, *Extremism on the Right* (New York: ADL, 1988), 84.

[64] Although it is not completely clear, it may be the case that the name was chosen to the ridicule or leverage the better-known NAACP (National Association for the Advancement of the Colored People).

[65] See, e.g., NAAWP, "Why is the NAAWP Necessary?," *NAAWP News*, July 66 (1992), 6.

[66] Mayer N. Zald and Bert Useem, "Movements and Counter Movements Interactions: Mobilization, Tactics and State Development," in ed. Mayer N. Zald and John D. McCarthy *Social Movements in and Organizational Society*, New Brunswick (New Jersey: Transaction, 1987), 247.

political gains, at least not on the national level.[67] Other KKK leaders experienced similar failures. Tom Metzger, for example, ran for a Senate seat in California in 1983 but was unable to garner more than three percent of the votes.[68] Frustrated by his inability to popularize his ideas via the conventional political mechanisms, he transformed his relatively mild *White American Political Association (WAPA)* into the *White Aryan Resistance (WAR)*, which in its heyday introduced the most extreme racist rhetoric to the far right landscape and encouraged its members to engage in militant, and sometimes violent, activities.[69] Hence, while in the 1920s the relatively mild posture of the KKK enabled it to ignite temporary mass support for the movement, these ideological maneuvers where much less effective in the 1970s and 1980s, or at least were not translated into formal political power.

In the early 1980s a new element joined the Klan and the neo-Nazi groups in populating the white supremacy landscape. The Skinhead subculture had initially developed in the UK in the late 1960s as an amalgam of delinquent white working class, anti-establishment activists protesting against the bourgeois influences in British culture, and ska/reggae/punk rock music and soccer fans;[70] all seeking to express their frustration at the harsh economic conditions and social marginalization of the British working class. Skinheads adopted a strident territorial and neighborhood identity, aggressive, often violent demeanor, and hostile views of consumer capital.[71]

British Skinheads of the early 1970s were influenced by working class concerns about the economic impact of the growing waves of immigrants to the United Kingdom and by the Conservative Party's anti-immigrant rhetoric regarding the threat of alien influence on British culture and lifestyle. They began to absorb white power ideology

---

[67] However, he was a short-term member of the Louisiana House after winning a special election by garnering 8459 votes in the 89th district.

[68] Dobratz and Shanks-Meile, 50.

[69] This is reflected very effectively in the words of Metzger himself: "with WAR…rather than trying to work with the System, as I had done with the WAPA, I shifted my stance and become more anti-system then ever…" Published originally in Tom Metzger, *Biography of Tom Metzger* (Fallbrook, California: WAR publication, 1996); see also Dobratz and Shanks-Meile, 50.

[70] Southern Poverty Law Center Intelligence Project, *Skinheads in America: racists on the rampage* (Southern Poverty Law Center publications: 2009?), 3.

[71] For the Stylistic dimensions of the skinheads subculture, see the following ethnographic study: Susan Willis, "Hardcore: Subculture American Style," *Critical Inquiry*, 19(2) (1993), 365–83.

and behavior, targeting immigrants, homosexuals and hippies.[72] The gradual shift of Skinhead groups to white power ideology further intensified in the late 1970s and early 1980s, and was reflected by two overlapping developments. First, references to Nazi heritage, symbols and memorabilia began to proliferate within the Skinhead subculture, in part due to influence of the punk music scene, which adopted Nazi symbols as a means of illustrating its anti-social, taboo-breaking nature.[73] Hence, the swastika, SS captions and other Nazi symbols became inherent aspects of Skinhead aesthetics. Second, ties were initiated between Skinhead groups and National Socialist organizations, in particular the British neo-Fascist Movement known as the *British National Front* (NF), which saw the Skinheads as a convenient recruitment source and was willing to provide them with financial and organizational assistance.[74] It is therefore not surprising that Skinhead violence assumed an anti-Semitic, anti-gay, anti-Communist and anti-immigrant outlook. In the mid and later parts of the 1980s Skinhead aesthetics spread across Europe, further enhancing its connections with the institutionalized European far right and further developing and nourishing a supportive cultural, mainly music, scene.[75]

The first seeds of the movement in the United States emerged in 1984–1985 with the appearance of extremist associations such as the Chicago-based *Romantic Violence* and the San Francisco-based *American Front*.[76] These associations perceived themselves as part of an American working class Aryan youth movement, opposing communist and capitalist elements, which they believed were aimed at undermining the superior status of the Aryan race in the United States.[77] Ideologically, the Skinheads held much in common with National Socialism, including intensive use of Nazi symbols and rhetoric. They also adopted most of the common rhetorical and ideological elements of veteran white supremacy groups, including radical nativism, support for ethnic internal

---

[72] Mark S. Hamm, *American Skinheads: The Criminology and Control of Hate Crime* (New York: Praeger, 1993), 23–5.

[73] Bruce Dancis, "Safety Pins and Class Struggle: Punk Rock and the Left," *Socialist Review* 8(39) (1978), 58–83; Dave Laing, *One Chord Wonders. Power and Meaning in Punk Rock* (New York: Open University Press, 1985); Hamm, 28–9.

[74] Jeff Coplon, "Skinheads Reich," *Utne Reader*, May/June (1989), 80–89.

[75] For what is likely to be the most comprehensive description of the movement, see Hamm.

[76] Southern Poverty Law Center report, *Skinheads in America* (unknown date), 3; ADL, *Hate Groups in America: A Record of Bigotry and Violence*, 2nd ed. (New York: ADL Publication, 1988); Coplon.

[77] Dobratz and Shanks-Meile, 64–7.

homogeneity and racist and exclusionary tendencies.[78] *Hammerskin Nation* is the largest Skinhead organization in the United States, and it serves as an umbrella organization for various Skinhead chapters spread all over the country. Its slogan—"We must secure the existence of our people and a future for White Children"[79]—embodies these ideological tendencies. It also reflects the youth-oriented nature of the movement, manifested in the Skinheads' strong emphasis on white power music as a cultural medium, fulfilling roles of recruitment, of formulating and influencing discourse, as well as functioning as a source of identification and solidarity.

To conclude, all three segments of SMOs of the racist movement are committed to the enhancement of internal homogeneity and to limiting foreign influence by engaging in practices based on exclusion, segregation, discriminatory policies and the spread of racist and discriminatory norms and values. Thus, what differentiates SMOs is not their aspirations, but their unique framing, target audience and historical references. This may explain why there is a relatively high level of cooperation between the SMOs of the racist movement, especially when compared with the relations between SMOs of other movements.

3.1.2 - Anti-Federalist Movement: Ideological Foundations

In contrast to the relatively long tradition of the white supremacy racist movement, the anti-federalist movement appeared in full force only in the early to mid-1990s, with the emergence of groups such as the *Militia of Montana* and the *Michigan Militia*. Anti-federalism is normally identified in the literature as the "Militia" or "Patriot" movement. Anti-federalist and anti-government sentiments were present in American society before the 1990s in diverse movements and ideological associations promoting anti-taxation, gun rights, survivalist practices,[80] and libertarian ideas. However, most scholars concur that the 1980s "farm crises," combined with the implications of rapid economic, cultural and technological changes in American society, growing political

---

[78] Southern Poverty Law Center report, *Skinheads in America* (Unknown Date): Hamm, 50–60.

[79] See, e.g., *Hammerskin Nation*, http://www.hammerskins.net/ (accessed 2 November 2012). The fourteen words were originally articulated by David Lane, a member of *The Order* who was involved with the assassination of Denver talk-radio celebrity Alan Berg and is now serving a life sentence. It should be mentioned also that the "Fourteen Words" also constitute an important part of the radical right's agenda for activists in Europe: see Jeffrey Kaplan ed. *Encyclopedia of White Power* (Walnut Creek CA: Altamira Press, 2000), p. 167.

[80] For compressive documentation of these groups see Daniel Levitas, *Terrorist Next Door, The Militia Movement and the Radical Right* (New York: St. Martin's press, 2003).

influences of minority groups, and attempts to revise gun control and environmental legislation, facilitated the rapid emergence of a cohesive movement in the mid to late 1990s.[81] In other words, the militia movement was a reactive social movement which mobilized in response to specific perceived threats.[82]

The anti-federalist movement's ideology is based on the idea that there is an urgent need to undermine the influence, legitimacy and practical sovereignty of the federal government and its proxy organizations.[83] The groups comprising the movement suggest several rationales that seek to legitimize anti-federal sentiments. Some groups are driven by a strong conviction that the American political system and its proxies were hijacked by external forces interested in promoting a "New World Order," (NWO) in which the United States will be embedded in the UN or another version of global government.[84] The NWO will be advanced, they believe, via steady transition of powers from local to federal law-enforcement agencies, i.e., the transformation of local police and law-enforcement agencies into a federally controlled "National Police" agency[85] that will in turn merge with a "Multi-National Peace Keeping Force."[86] The latter deployment on US soil will be justified via a domestic campaign implemented by interested parties that will emphasize American society's deficiencies and US government incompetency. This will convince the American people that restoring stability and order inevitably demands the use of international forces. The last stage, according to most NWO narratives, involves the transformation of the United States government into an international/world government and the execution and oppression

---

[81] See e.g., Richard Abanes, *American Militias*. Downers Grove (Illinois: Intervarsity Press, 1996), 7–20; Joel Dyer, *Harvest of Rage* (Bolder, Colorado: Westview Press, 1998), 24–44; Kathlyn Gay, *Militias: Armed and Dangerous* (Springfield, New Jersey: Enslow Publishers INC., 1997), 36–52; Nella Van Dyke and A. Sarah Soule, "Structural Social Changes and the Mobilizing Effect of Threat: Explaining Levels of Patriot and Militia Organizing in the United States," *Social Problems*, 49(4) (2002), 497–520.

[82] See Van Dyke and Soule, 497–520; for an example of strain theories see also Daniel Bell, "The Disposed-1962," in Daniel Bell ed. *The Radical Right* (Garden City, New York: Doubleday and Co., 1962), 1–38; Joseph Gusfield, *Symbolic Crusade and the American Temperance Movement* (Urbana and Chicago, Illinois: University of Illinois Press, 1963).

[83] Abanes; Dyer; Gay, 36–52.

[84] Martin Durham, "American Far Right and 9/11," *Terrorism and Political Violence* 15(2) (2003), 96–111.

[85] Some use the term "Multi-Jurisdictional Task Force" or MJTF: see e.g., Mark Koernke, "America in Peril," *Liveleak* (Real World Publication, 1993), http://www.liveleak.com/view?comments=1&i=be2_1269967024 (accessed 2 November 2012).

[86] See e.g., George Eaton, "America is Lost Because the People are Lost," *Patriot Report*, 2 October (1994); Jack Mclamb, *Operation Vampire Killer 2000* (Phoenix: PATNWO, 2000), 3.

of those opposing this process.[87] Linda Thompson, the head of the *Unorganized Militia of the United States*[88] details the consequence of this global coup: "This is the coming of the New World Order. A one-world government, where, in order to put the new government in place, we must all be disarmed first. To do that, the government is deliberately creating schisms in our society, funding both the anti-abortion/pro-choice sides, the antigun/pro-gun issues…trying to provoke a riot that will allow martial law to be implemented and all weapons seized, while 'dissidents' are put safely away".[89] The fear of the materialization of the NWO makes most militias not merely hostile towards the federal government but also hostile towards international organizations, whether non-profitable NGOs, international corporations, or political institutions of the international community, such as the UN.[90]

The militias' anti-federalist sentiments are also rationalized by their perception of the corrupted and tyrannical nature of the federal government and its apparent tendency to violate individuals' civilian liberties and constitutional rights.[91] That is why they are concerned about the transformation of the United States into a police state in which

---

[87] Richard Abens, *American Militias* (Downers Grove, Illinois: Intervarsity Press, 1996), 75–86.

[88] It should be noted that Thompson, who regards herself as "Adjunct General of the *Unorganized Militia of the United States*" is one of more prolific ideologists of the Patriot movement: see Neil A. Hamilton, *Militias in America* (Santa Barbara, California: ABC-CLIO Inc., 1996), 35–7.

[89] Linda Thompson, "Waco, Another Perspective," *American Justice Foundation Publications* (unknown date), http://www.skeptictank.org/files/waco/ltstory2.htm (accessed 2 November 2012). Other less popular versions crowd the far right landscape, e.g., (unknown author), "Conspiracy? What Concipiracy?" *New Jersey Newsletter*, 1 September (1995) : "The New World Order (NWO) is simply this: all nations that have nuclear weapons will turn them over to UN control, thus making the UN Supreme Military Power on earth; and no nation, including the US, would have the military might to wage war. United States sovereignty, along with the sovereignty of other nations, will come to an end."

[90] As an example, in December 1994 during the "Patriot Alert Rally" in Brevard county in Florida, Militia members protested against flying the UN flag at the city hall; another example can be found in *Operation Vampire Killer 2000*, one of the most popular texts among Militia members, which was produced by the *American Citizens and Lawmen Association in Arizona*, and focuses on uncovering elements interested in ending US independency. Honorable place among the Vampires is kept for the UN: see American Citizens and Lawmen Association in Arizona, *Operation Vampire Killer 2000*, (Phoenix: Police against the New World Order, 1992).

[91] See e.g., regarding the Second Amendment, Militia of Montana, *Militia of Montana Information and Networking Manual*, (1994), 2: "False is the idea of utility…that would take fire from men because it burns and water because one may drown in it; that has no remedy for evils except destruction (of liberty). The laws that forbid the carrying of arms are laws of such nature. They disarm only those who are neither inclined nor determined to commit crimes…"

power is used arbitrarily and without accountability.[92] In the words of a *Missouri Militia* member, "One of the things that people really fear from the government is the idea that the government can ruin your life; totally destroy your life….split your family up, do the whole thing and walk off like you're a discarded banana peel, and with a ho-hum attitude."[93]

In the context of violation of constitutional rights, militia members in particular tend to point out the steady increase in gun control and environmental legislation and the overregulation of the economic and social realms, especially in regard to immigration and education issues. The opposition to gun control legislation has been driven mainly by the perception of many that this represents a breach of the Second Amendment and a direct violation of a constitutional right, having direct impact on the ability of many to preserve their common practices and way of life. In contrast, the opposition to environmental legislation has been driven by the economic consequences of this legislation, as perceived by the militia members, in particular the decline of industries which are not environmentally friendly but crucial for the economy in rural areas. The Testimony of Susan Schock reveals the resulting frustration, clearly expressed in the words of Charles Shumway, *Arizona Militia* member: "Unless the 'curse' of the Endangered Species Act was repealed, there would be 'rioting, bloodshed, rebellion and conflict that will make the Serbian-Bosnia affair look like a Sunday picnic.'"[94]

Finally, many of the militias also legitimize their ideological tendencies by referring to the strong role of civilian activism, civilian paramilitary groups, individual freedoms, and self-governing and frontier culture in America's history and ethos, especially during the Revolutionary War and the expansion to the West.[95] Hence, members of these groups see themselves as the successors of the nation's founding fathers, and as

---

[92] Stephen Vertigans, "Beyond the Fringe? Radicalization within the American Far Right," *Totalitarian Movements and Political Religions,* 8(3–4) (2007), 641–59.

[93] Robert L. Snow, *Terrorists Among Us: The Militia Threat* (Cambridge, Massachusetts: Perseus Publishing, 1999), 27.

[94] Testimony of Susan Schock, Director of Gila Watch, in front of the Montana House of representatives, 11 July, 1995, http://www.clintonlibrary.gov/_previous/KAGAN%20COUNSEL/Counsel%20-%20Box%20032%20-%20Folder%20009.pdf (accessed 2 November 2012).

[95] For a comprehensive discussion of the relation between US early history and the contemporary militia movement, see Darren Mulloy, *American Extremism: History, Politics and Militia Movement* (New York: Routledge, 2004).

part of a struggle to restore or preserve what they regard as America's true identity, values and way of life.[96]

To conclude, it should be noted that historically some of the anti-federalist groups have absorbed racist and Christian Identity sentiments; nonetheless, the glue binding their membership and driving their activism has been and remains hostility, fear and the need to challenge or restrict the sovereignty of the federal government.

3.1.3 - Christian Fundamentalist Movement: Ideological Foundations

The Christian fundamentalist violent far right emerged from two ideological platforms. The more influential and popular one is that of the Christian Identity school of thought. The second is the anti-abortion/pro-life paradigm. Hence, the ideological pillars of both are the main theme of the current section.

3.1.3.1 – Ideological Tenets of the Christian Identity Movement

Christian Identity groups combine religious fundamentalism with traditional white supremacy racist ideology. With the promotion of ideas of nativism, exclusionism, and internal homogeneity, these groups advocate racial superiority via idiosyncratic interpretations of religious texts that focus on the division of humanity according to primordial attributes.[97] More specifically, they maintain an interpretation of holy texts which is meant to support the notion that it is not the people of Israel but Anglo-Saxons who are the chosen people.[98] Moreover, they maintain that a Manichaean war between evil and good is central to the Bible and will be manifested in racial war between the white Anglo-Saxon nation and various non-Anglo-Saxon ethnic groups such as the "Children of Satan" (Jews) and "mud-people" (non-whites).[99] The Identity groups tend to rely on spurious religious heritage, symbols, rituals and norms in order to instill and spread these ideas. They also use such symbols and rituals to provide encouragement

---

[96] Ibid.

[97] For a comprehensive review of the movement's ideological framework, see Michael Barkun, *Religion and the Racist Right* (Chapel Hill and London: University of North Carolina Press, 1994); Robert Charles, *Race over Grace: The Racialist Religion of the Christian Identity Movement* (Lincoln, Nebraska: iUniverse, 2003); Walter Jerome, *One Aryan Nation Under God: Exposing the New Racial Extremists* (Cleveland, Ohio: Pilgrim Press, 2000).

[98] See e.g., Dan Gayman, *Do all Races Share in Salvation? For Whom Did Jesus Christ Die?* (Schell City, Missouri: The Church of Israel, 1995).

[99] Sheldon Emry, *Hairs of Promise* (Phoenix: Lord's Covenant Church, unknown date), 25; Jerome; 34–5.

and moral justification for political activism against perceived threats to their preferred socio-political order.[100]

The ideological roots of the American Christian Identity movement can be traced to mid-nineteenth century England and the writings and lectures of a radical Scottish weaver by the name of John Wilson. Wilson advocated the idea that the lost biblical Israeli tribes migrated from the Middle East and settled in northern Europe, eventually constituting the current Anglo-Saxon nations.[101] Since the implication is that the Anglo-Saxons are the chosen people, the "British Israelites" (or "Anglo-Israelism") believe that Anglo-Saxons are charged with a divine duty to conquer, dominate and colonize the earth in the spirit of the biblical prophesies believed to have been given originally to the people of Israel.[102] In the late 1860s and 1870s, bank clerk Edward Hine was influenced by Wilson's writings and became a major force in spreading these ideas throughout the British Isles and ultimately the United States with an effective network of publications and associations which promoted the principles of the British Israelites. Hine refined these writings to express the growing Anglo-American anti-German sentiment.[103]

In the late nineteenth and early twentieth centuries several branches of this theological movement were established on the East Coast of the United States, mainly under the umbrella of the *British-Israelite World Federation*. This American wing expanded steadily before the Second World War while gradually embracing anti-Semitic and racial rhetoric.[104] These developments are generally attributed to the early leaders of the movement's American wing, William J. Cameron and Howard Rand, who

---

[100] In most cases the ideologists of the identity movement will supplement the 66 canonical books of the New and Old Testament with readings from apocryphal books. Their approach to the Bible is typified by the following statement of the Kingdom Identity ministers: "We believe the entire bible, both Old and New Testaments, as originally inspired, to be inerrant, supreme, revealed word of God…all scripture is written as doctrinal standard for our exhortation, admonition, correction, instruction, and example, the whole counsel to be believed, taught, and followed." See Jerome, 49; and "Doctrinal Statement of Belief" (Merrimac, Masschusetts: Destiny Publishers), 3.

[101] His most important work was published in 1840: see John Wilson, *Lectures on Our Israelitish Origin* (London: James Nisbet, 1840).

[102] John Wilson, "British Idealism: The ideological Restraints on Sect Organization," in Bryan R. Wilson ed. *Patterns of Sectarianism: Organization and Ideology in Social and Religious Movements* (London: Heinemann, 1967).

[103] Barkun, 6–15.

[104] David A. Gerber, "Anti-Semitism and Jewish-Gentile Relations in American Historiography and the American Past," in David. A. Gerber (Ed) *Anti-Semitism in American History* (Urbana: University of Illinois Press, 1986), 20–22.

systematically identified the Zionist movement and Jews as the main enemies of the British-Israelite movement and engaged in anti-Semitic activities and propaganda.

Cameron and Rand's followers after WWII, especially the preachers Gerald K. Smith, Wesley Swift, Richard Butler and William Potter Gale, continued to develop the British-Israelite ideological paradigm in their respective Identity churches and groups (such as *Church of Jesus Christ Christian*, and *The US Christian Posse Association*), consistently employing theological analysis to further proselytize extreme anti-Semitism, notions of white supremacy and racial segregation, and to exult in apocalyptic visions, transforming the British Israelites into the current day Identity movement.

The Identity movement's anti-Semitic tendencies were not merely a result of its identification of the Jews as the direct biological offspring of Satan (the rationale for which will be explained later in this section), but also a reflection of several representations and perceptions of the Jews, which appeared systematically in the writing and preaching of the movement's leaders. The first is the idea of Jewish world conspiracy. Citing the "Protocols of the Elders of Zion" as symbolic proof, Identity leaders today promote the belief that Jewish dominance of financial arenas all over the world is a means of instigating the destruction of Aryan civilizations.[105] Secondly, Identity thinkers criticize Jewish claims to be the chosen race by averring that the Jewish peoples are actually the descendants of Judah, the least advanced and the most primitive of the ancient biblical tribes, and not one of the ten lost tribes of Israel.[106] Finally, Identity ideology tends to describe Judaism as the prevailing threat to the Anglo-Saxon race and the Identity movement, as illustrated in the following statement of an Identity thinker:

> The wicked of the earth, the enemies of Christ, have grown strong and arrogant in our land. They have infiltrated our schools, news media, churches and government in their attempts to keep you in ignorance of your

---

[105] See e.g., (unknown author), "Gentile Fall Involved in Hope of Jewish Rule," *Dearborn Independent*: 8–9. Many similar examples exist in the written universe of the movement. For further analysis see also Barkun, 34–9.

[106] Some of them even go further, arguing that the Jews are the descendants of a mix of ethnic groups,; this is evident in the words of an identity thinker: "A Vast majority of Those calling themselves Jews Today are descendants from the Canaanites, Edomites, Mongolians…while these people call themselves Jews, The Bible Makes clear that they are of the Synagogue of Satan". See Dan Gyman, *Two Seeds of Genesis, 3:15 rev* (Schell City, Missouri: Church of Israel, 1994), 7; see also the same argument in William Potter Gale's "The Fate of our Fathers," *Identity* 7(1974), 1.

identity as Israelites. They are attempting to steal your heritage. The heritage their father Esau despised and sold; that they might conquer America and take rule over the whole earth, and destroy, if they can, the very name of Christ, Christians and Christianity. But God Almighty has decreed the destruction of those who hate Jesus Christ and His True Israel People [Obadiah 18].[107]

Historically, other anti-Semitic characteristics have emerged in the movement, including Holocaust denial and the linking of Jews to practices and beliefs which their members perceive to be socially injurious, such as abortion and socialism.[108]

While anti-Semitism is the most recognized ideological feature of the Identity movement, an apocalyptic belief that the world/history is in its last days is at least as important a component in the Identity paradigm. Already in the late 1890s and early decades of the twentieth century, millenarian perceptions dominated the British-Israelite movement. Hine indicated several stages which would lead to the "second coming of the Lord," including restoration of the Jews, i.e. their adoption of Christianity; the universal acceptance of the gospel; and the resurrection of the faithful.[109] In later decades, other Identity scholars promoted different visions and historical narratives regarding the path which would eventually end with the second coming and the restoration of the dominance of the true people of Israel. Most of them emphasized that the superior and unique status of the Aryan race is a directive of God, and that the war between the children of light and of darkness (non Aryans) has already begun and will cease with divine intervention and the establishment of Christ's Kingdom. Many of these supernatural forecasts also incorporate topical historical conflicts such as the Cold War, the Israeli-Arab conflict, or other events which have signaled the coming collapse of the existing world order.

---

[107] Willie Martin, "The Assyrians Who Took The Israelites Captive Did Not Call Them By That Name!" Part 7 of 32 (Chapter Five), *In Search of Isaac's Children*, see http://www.fathersmanifesto.net/wm/wm0170/wm0170g.html (accessed 2 November 2012).
[108] These tendencies apparently could also be identified in the broader pro-Life movement, as the words of Father Paul Marx, founder of "Human Life International," illustrate: "it is a strange thing how many leaders of the abortion movement are Jewish." See Aryeh Dean Cohen, "ADL: Anti-abortion attacks tainted with anti-Semitism", *Jerusalem Post Service*, (1998), see http://www.jweekly.com/article/full/9450/adl-anti-abortion-attacks-tainted-with-anti-semitism/ (accessed 2 November 2012).
[109] Barkun, 79–81.

The third ideological pillar of the Identity movement is the endorsement of racial segregation and the notion of the superiority of the Aryan race. The origins of these perceptions are embedded in the Identity movement's interpretation of the biblical story of Genesis. According to this version, Adam was not the first man, but the first white man. Before him, pre-Adamic people of color were created by God who possessed lesser spiritual attributes and qualities.[110] Furthermore, the white people could be divided into two competing "seed-lines": those who are descendants of Adam and Eve (Aryans), and all others (non-Aryans), who are descendants of Eve and the serpent.[111] Based on this interpretation, the Identity thinkers concluded that race mixing, as in the case of Eve and the serpent, was the original sin that led to the expulsion of the white man from the Garden of Eden.[112] The narrative identifies Cain, the first murderer, as the son of Satan and the first Jew.[113]

The exploitation of biblical texts to promulgate racial and other ideological notions is a common practice in the ideological construction of the Identity movement. Another example is the Identity movement's interpretation of God's revelations to Abraham and his sons of the transformation of Israel into a dominant, flourishing and powerful nation as an indication of the destiny of the Aryan people. Two further related trends are worth mentioning. The first is the use of apocryphal historical revisionism to associate each architectural achievement of ancient times to the white race, i.e., Egypt's

---

[110] See e.g., from the *Kingdom Identity Ministry's* "Doctrinal Statement of Belief": "We believe that the man *Adam* (a Hebrew word meaning: ruddy, to show blood, flush, turn rosy, is father of the White race only. As son of God, made in his likeness, Adam and his descendants, who are also the children of God, can know YHVH god as their creator…"; Dan Gyman, and by proxy, *the Church of Israel*, provides a detailed analysis of the Biblical text in order to rationalize this perspective: "without being dogmatic, if the Bible includes the record of how the Non-Adamic were created, it is found in Genesis 1:25, where the Chay Neffesh or living creatures are named. The living creatures here could have been biped or quadruped…the Chai Neffesh creation, if it does include the other races, means they were created by Yahweh…" and "Adam is the particularized creation. While Yahweh obviously created other races separately, the bible makes no efforts to detail this creation because it was not intended to be the family history of any other race than Adam kind". See Gyman (1955), 150.
[111] Charles, 31–7.
[112] Since all races were created as different "functions", it is a sin to promote in race mixing. M'Causland, for example, who had significant influence on identity thinkers, argues that the flood was punishment as a direct consequence of racial mixing: "it is plain that the moving cause of the destruction of the Adamites, with the exception of Noah's family was that their race had become corrupted by the admixture of non-adamite blood." See Dominick M'causland, *Adam and the Adamite* (London: Richard Bently and Son, 1872), 70; for a more systematic analysis see also Chester L. Quarles, *Christian Identity: The Aryan American Bloodline Religion* (Jefferson: North Carolina, McFarland and Company, 2004), 89–91.
[113] Barkun, 162–3.

Middle Kingdom pyramids, Wiltshire's Neolithic post-and-lintel structure of Stonehenge, or the 17th century Mughal mausoleum, the Taj Mahal. The second is the inclination to associate the non-Aryan seed-line with anti-Christian historical events, in particular the persecution and murder of Jesus.[114]

To conclude, the ideological landscape of the Identity movement is continuing to develop as prominent Christian Identity associations have continued to emerge in recent decades. Worth noting were Robert Miles' *Mountain Church of Jesus Christ*, which introduced the concept of Dualism[115] and further integrated ideas of racial purity and genetic cleansing into the familiar Christian Identity narrative; James K. Warner's *New Christian Crusade Church*, which expanded the Identity racial rhetoric to target immigrant groups; and the *The LaPorta Church of Christ*, which made an effort to present a milder, less militant version of Christian Identity under the leadership of Pete Peters.[116]

3.1.3.2 – Ideological Tenets: Violent Anti-Abortionist Groups

As mentioned, the Identity movement was not the only source of far-right violence based on religious fundamentalism; since the late 1970s Americans have witnessed an increase in the number of violent attacks against the abortion industry, which have been initiated by groups and individuals demonstrating strong religious and fundamentalist sentiments.

While the current study cannot cover the many different facets of the struggle between the American pro-life and pro-choice movements, it should nonetheless be noted that almost from its early days, and definitely after the 1973 Supreme Court ruling in *Roe v. Wade*, religious views have been significant, if not a major part, of pro-life ideological construction. It is no coincidence that the pro-life leadership has been dominated by religious leaders and associations. For example, the American Catholic leadership invested significant efforts in thwarting the growing impact of the *Roe v. Wade* Supreme

---

[114] See for example "White Camelia Knights of the Ku Klux Klan," http://www.wckkkk.org/identity.html (accessed 2 November 2012); for further examples see also Jerome, 82–5; Barkun, 121–98.

[115] Dualism existed before the Christian era and is manifested in a struggle between God and his Angels, and Satan. It presents minor differences to the story of how Eve was seduced in Eden in order to create the children of Satan, and that the Anglo-Saxons descended to earth in Europe rather than being the descendants of the lost Israeli tribes.

[116] See also Dobratz and Shanks-Meile, 80–81.

Court decision and in 1974 the United States Catholic Conference sent four cardinals to Washington, DC in order to convince Congress to legislate a national prohibition on abortion.[117] At the same time, other associations with orthodox orientations, such as *Life Amendment Political Action Committee, Committee for the Survival of a Free Congress* and *Committee for Pro-Life Affairs* promoted a pro-life agenda via engagement in electoral processes, usually by focusing on thwarting the election of pro-choice candidates.[118]

Gradually, some pro-life leaders stretched the religious pro-life rationale into the realms of Manichaean dualism[119] and fundamentalist militancy, which are familiar from the ideological rhetoric of the Identity movement. During 1979, for example, two well-known speakers of the evangelical movement at that time, Dr. C. Everett Koop and Francis Schaeffer, consistently claimed during a speaking tour that *Roe v. Wade* "symbolize[d] the triumph of evil over good."[120] The implications were not late in appearing, when a number of individuals engaged in militant activism to promote this view. For instance, on 15 February 1979 twenty-one year old Peter Burkin ignited a gasoline can in a nonprofit abortion clinic in Hempstead, New York. In the following years, similar attacks were perpetrated, mostly by individuals affiliated with the *Army of God (AOG)*, the organization which would become the public face of the violent campaign against abortion clinics and their staffs during the 1980s and 1990s.[121]

While the operational characteristics of *AOG* will be discussed later in this study, its manual, which was uncovered in 1993 in the backyard of one of its activists, Shelly Shannon, allows a unique glimpse into the ideological principles of pro-life violence. First, those who support abortion are representatives of the devil and evil; hence, pro-life forces must acknowledge that their struggle is part of an ongoing war between Satan and God's children.[122] Second, the abortion industry is perceived as no less than a mechanism for the systematic killing of innocent and pure human beings, or as it is

---

[117] Connie Paige, *Right to Lifers* (New York: Summit Books, 1983), 60.

[118] Patricia Baird-Windle and Eleanor J. Bader, *Targets of Hatred: Anti Abortion Terrorism* (New York: Palgrave, 2001), 41.

[119] Charles, 31–7.

[120] Frank Schaeffer, "We Who Sowed Hate Share Blame In Killing Of Abortion Doctor," *Baltimore Sun*, (2 June 2009), http://articles.baltimoresun.com/2009-06-02/news/0906010039_1_abortion-late-term-roe-v (accessed 2 November 2012); Baird-Windle and Bader, 61–62.

[121] Joni Scott, "From Hate Rhetoric to Hate Crimes: A Link Acknowledged Too Late," *Humanist*, January/February (1999), 3.

[122] "The Army of God: Dedication," *Army of God Manual* (author unknown), Third Edition, chapter 1, http://www.armyofgod.com/AOGsel1.html (accessed 2 November 2012).

described, a "new Holocaust."[123] Third, since every human being is created in the image of God, it is by definition a sin to end their lives before they have been able to "enjoy love and life of this planet."[124] Fourth, those who participate actively in the pro-life war are members of a clandestine avant-garde, regarded as a remnant, a small minority among the communities of believers. The reason for that is that the fragmentation of the Christian religious establishment prevents any likelihood of unity behind the cause of preventing abortion. Finally, the use of violence in this cause has several objectives: (a) demolishing the murder weapons, i.e., destroying the structure within which abortions are being committed; (b) disarming the individuals responsible for or participating in the crimes by inflicting severe physical harm on them; (c) to deter those who continue to engage in and to be part of the abortion industry by advocating the view that "the only rational way to respond to the knowledge of an imminent and brutal murder is direct action."[125] Hence, the violence is an act of rescue or defensive action rather than of murder;[126] (d) lastly, the violence aims to ignite the public discourse regarding the morality of abortion. As explained in the *AOG Manual*:

> It is easy at this time for the media as a whole to hold the position that they do: they can comfortably be for death. Not so when the honorable citizens of any given community begin to rise up in righteous indignation and destroy these miniature Dachaus. All of a sudden, apathy is gone. The average reporter says to himself, 'Wow! Maybe there are a few people that really believe all this jargon about abortion being murder.'[127]

To conclude, pro-life violence is driven by several ideological building blocks that are enhanced by religious-based convictions, i.e., fetuses are human beings created in God's image, and as such should be accorded the rights of humans from the moment of conception; any violent acts to end their lives are immoral and should be prevented. Prevention includes damaging the physical tools of the crime, as well as shaping a

---

[123] Operation B.R.I.C.K.: Babies Rescued Through Increased Cost Of Killing," *Army of God Manual*. Third edition, chapter 1: http://www.armyofgod.com/AOGsel3.html (accessed 2 November 2012).
[124] Ibid.
[125] Danny W. Davis, *The Phinehas Priesthood: Violent Vanguard of the Christian Identity Movement* (Greenwood Publishing Group, Praeger: Santa Barbara, California, 2010), 111.
[126] "An interview with an underground leader of the American Holocaust Resistance Movement," *Army of God Manual*. Third edition, http://www.armyofgod.com/AOGsel7.html (accessed 2 November 2012).
[127] Ibid.

moral and political environment which will convince people of the immorality of the abortion industry and deter people from becoming part of it.

3.2 - *Structural and Operational Patterns within the American Far Right, 1865–2000s*

In order to provide an overview of the organizational and operational characteristics of the violent far right, there is a need to differentiate between two distinct levels of analysis. The first refers to the structural-operational patterns within the broad Social Movements comprising the far-right arena (i.e., Racist/White Supremacy, Anti-federalist, Christian-fundamentalist), while the second relates to structural-operational patterns within the specific SMOs (organizations comprising the different far-right movements). The following sections will address both levels of analysis.

3.2.1 - *Racist/White Supremacy Movement: Organizational and Operational Evolution*

Initial analysis of more than 150 years of political activism reveals several cyclical trends within the white supremacy movement. In terms of their popularity, the groups comprising this movement have enjoyed several peaks in their lifespan which were usually followed by relatively quick and dramatic declines. Thus, mobilization and growth was almost never a continuous long-term gradual process, but rather a response to specific historical processes or events and social-political conditions which were used by capable political entrepreneurs.[128] The latter rarely were able to maintain the attractiveness or significance of their organization and ideology in the face of changing political conditions. So, for example, while the KKK was able to exploit economic and social conditions several times in order to enhance its relevancy, it was almost never able to adapt when the environment became less favorable. While this corresponds with existing organizational and political violence literature, which tends to distinguish between a group's adaptability and its durability, it still raises the question of the specific factors which prevented the white supremacy movement groups from developing effective mechanisms of adaptation, especially since some of the groups affiliated with other movements were more successful in this regard. While these kinds of questions will be discussed further in the theoretical-empirical section of this study, it should be noted that trends in popularity have also been reflected in the level of violence produced by the different groups, as a rise in numbers of members has

---

[128] This corresponds with some aspects of Political Opportunity Structure and mobilization theories, which will be further discussed in the empirical section of this study.

consistently been reflected by a rise in the level of violence, even in cases when the leadership objected to violent practices. This increase in violence despite leadership proscription confirms the inherently violent and militant nature of the movement, but it also implies an incapacity in maintaining operational discipline in times of organizational growth. Furthermore, it affirms the validity of theoretical frameworks linking growth in the level of social interactions within groups with escalation in the militancy of organizational practices.

Finally, it appears that in many of the groups, repeated attempts by the organizational leadership to enforce a rigid hierarchical structure have been relatively unsuccessful, and have eventually led to the opposite result, i.e., increased fragmentation of the group or movement. The following sections, examining the various groups which were active within the racist movement, further discuss these tendencies and provide an explanatory theoretical basis which will be developed in the theoretical-empirical section of this study.

3.2.1.1 – Ku Klux Klan (KKK)

One of the earliest manifestations of far-right political activism in the United States was the first generation KKK, which emerged in the American south during the second half of the 1860s and early 1870s. Structurally and organizationally, its short history can be divided into two distinct eras, before and after the first KKK convention. Between December 1865 and April 1867 the movement spread across the South, growing quickly with chapters established in Alabama, Mississippi, Kentucky, Virginia, West Virginia, South Carolina and Georgia. A limited level of coordination and cooperation was maintained between the different regional Klans, and a central leadership was nonexistent.[129] The first attempt to institutionalize the movement was made during the first convention of the KKK in Nashville, Tennessee during April 1867, when Ret. General Nathan Bedford Forrest was appointed as the first national leader of the movement: the "Grand Wizard." It was decided that the imperial headquarters would be based in Memphis. Under his leadership, what was referred to as the "Invisible Empire" was divided into realms (under the leadership of "Grand Dragons"),

---

[129] Quarles (1999), 43.

dominions (under the leadership of "Grand Titans"), provinces (under the leadership of "Grand Giants") and Dens (under the leadership of "Grand Cyclops").[130]

Despite attempts to consolidate an established hierarchy, evidence shows that this had a limited effect on the operational characteristics of the movement, with the different regional branches remaining highly independent, both in terms of the freedom to choose the type of activities they preferred to undertake and their selection of targets for attack. Most groups had a very flat internal structure, with each rank-and-file member of the movement (a "Ghoul") usually given a title based on his specific role.[131] The fragmented nature seems to have been a result of the limited logistical capacity of the leadership to monitor the operations of the different regional branches effectively; the zealous local sentiment of the activists, who usually believed they knew best how to enforce their values in their town or province; and the tendency of Bedford himself to empower the local associations of the KKK.[132]

Violent manifestations of the KKK at that time were directed mainly against African Americans, representatives of northern-based organizations, and local individuals involved in social interracial activities.[133] While some of the Klan chapters claimed to focus on regulation rather than punishment, violence was a recurring component in most regional Klan activities.[134] To illustrate, the Tennessee Klan alone was involved in the early fall and summer of 1867 in 140 violent incidents; 25 of them ended with fatalities and 35 included extreme assaults.[135] Many of the latter involved branding of their victims or mutilation with acid, flogging and physical beating. While these kinds of activities encouraged the perception in the North that the KKK was a violent subversive group, in the South many still viewed these activities as patriotic retribution.[136] This was also reflected in the growing popularity of the movement in that region. While there is no clear evidence regarding the size of the overall movement at

---

[130] David Chalmers, *Hooded Americanism* (New York: Doubleday, 1965), 181.

[131] Chalmers, 13–19.

[132] Quarles (1999), 43.

[133] As an example, Randel mentions that 74 people were killed at that time in Georgia, and 109 in Alabama: see William Pierce Randel, *Ku Klux Klan: A Century of Infamy* (Philadelphia, PA: Chilton, 1965), 114.

[134] Susan Lawrence Davis, *Authentic History, 1865-1877* (New York: American Library Service, 1924), 15–16.

[135] Martin Gitlin, *Ku Klux Klan* (Santa Barbara, California: ABC-CLIO, 2009), 5.

[136] Quarles (1999), 39.

that time, Forrest claimed in an 1868 interview that the Tennessee Klan included more than 40,000 members and that the overall number of KKK members in the South was over half a million.[137] It is unclear how reliable these numbers are, but there is broad consensus that at that time much of the white population in the South felt empathy towards the KKK.[138]

Ironically, the rapid expansion and the fragmented structure of the first KKK were the primary causes for its ultimate collapse. While the cellular structure of the movement provided flexibility and helped to overcome ideological and operational disagreements between different regional Klans, it also crippled the leadership's ability to enforce movement-wide practices and policies when necessary. Hence, despite the fact that in late 1869 and early 1870 the federal authorities intensified their pressure against KKK violence, small cells of the movement all over the South continued to engage in brutal attacks against African Americans and white supporters of African-American rights.[139] This in turn further legitimized federal scrutiny and legal actions against the Klan. Eventually, after acknowledging the limited authorization and control he had over the different chapters of the KKK, and facing federal chargers, Forrest announced the disbandment of the KKK in January 1869.[140] The violence continued until the end of 1871 when a combination of military, administrative and legal measures led to the gradual decomposition of most regional Klans.[141]

Growing anti-immigrant sentiment following the extensive waves of immigration to urban America in the late nineteenth and early twentieth centuries, combined with the immense impact of the influential film *the Birth of a Nation*, led several Atlanta based entrepreneurs, headed by Colonel William Simons, to reestablish the KKK in 1915.[142]

---

[137] "Interview with Nathan Bedford Forrest," *Wikisource*, The Free Library, http://en.wikisource.org/w/index.php?title=Interview_with_Nathan_Bedford_Forrest&oldid=3853811 (accessed November 2, 2012).

[138] For further details concerning first generation KKK see also Chalmers, 1–22; Horn; William Loren Katz, *The Invisible Empire: The Ku Klux Klan Impact on History* (Washington, DC: Open Hand, 1986); J. C. Lester and D. L. Wilson, *Ku Klux Klan, Its Origin, Growth, and Disbandonment* (Nashville, Tennessee: Walter Lynwood Fleming, 1884).

[139] As described by the Grand Dragon Forrest himself "The South has become a veritable hell through misrule": see Quarles (1999), 45.

[140] Gitlin, 7.

[141] To illustrate, between July and December 1871 around 1,700 KKK klansmen were arrested in the states of South Carolina, North Carolina, Mississippi and Georgia. See Newton and Newton, 335.

[142] For more on the circumstances that led to the reestablishment of the KKK see Rice, iii; Randel, 181.

The Birth of a Nation depicted the heroic role of the KKK during the Reconstruction era as the protector of white people from African-American violence. In a similar vein, the KKK exploited the growing popularity of the printed media for publication and distribution of its propaganda via the services of the public relations firm Southern Publicity Association (SPA), which helped to promulgate the message using a variety of media platforms.[143] Also relying on a pyramid recruiting system,[144] Simons and his associates were able to mobilize support from the breadth of the South, increasing the number of members from several hundred in 1915 to several million in the mid-1920s—estimations range from 1.1 million to close to 5 million members.[145]

Following WWI, the KKK gradually succeeded in establishing chapters in the North. Several factors were responsible for its growing popularity in this region of the country, including returning African-American soldiers' dissatisfaction with their marginalization in American society and massive immigration of African Americans to the North. Both of these trends added to the tensions in class and racial relations in many urban centers, especially in the Northeast.[146] Increasing discontent caused by postwar immigration and its effect on the labor market and other structural economic changes were to the KKK's advantage as well.[147] Added to this, the relatively mild image of the KKK, perceived by many at that time as an "American Movement" focused on national issues, helped in this regard.[148] Each of these aspects created a convenient environment for the transformation of the new KKK into a mass movement.

Organizationally, Simmons adopted the hybrid structure of the original KKK for the revised movement which, while including a rigid formal hierarchy, also provided

---

[143] It became eventually the propaganda Department of the KKK.

[144] Henry P. Fry, *Modern Ku Klux Klan* (New York: Negro University Press, 1922), 16.

[145] Stanley Frost, *Challenges of the Klan* (New York: Negro University Press, 1924), 238: Frost argued that the KKK included more than 4 million members, even though the PSLC documentation indicates 5 million: Southern Poverty Law Center Klanwatch Staff, *Ku Klux Klan: A History of Racism and Violence* ed. Susan Ballard, (Montgomery, Alabama: SPLC Publication, 1988), 46. McVeigh also provides strong evidence of the growing dominance of the Klan in many Midwest and northern regions of the United States, emphasizing strong empathy towards the organization, even by non-members. For example, he mentions that more than two thirds of the cities in the US with a population above 50,000 experienced KKK activities: see Rory McVeigh, 3, 12–13.

[146] Isabel Wilkerson, *The Warmth of Other Suns: The Epic Story of America's Great Migration* (New York: Vintage, 2011).

[147] Quarles (1999), 43–53.

[148] Rory McVeigh, 5–7.

significant freedom to the regional Klans. The Imperial Wizard was assisted by 15 imperial officers ("Kloncilium") and a legislative body ("Klonvokation") consisting of the imperial officers, special elected delegates and Grand Dragons.[149] The latter were appointed to lead particular realms (states); the realms in turn were divided into provinces where several regional Klans could potentially operate, each in its own "Klanton."

Simmons also introduced an effective financial model which helped to sustain and expand the new organization. It consisted of two main elements: the first was the pyramid-like recruiting model. It was based on a network of recruiters (mainly "Kleagles" and Protestant ministers) who were paid a fixed percentage of the initiation fee ($10) for each recruit they brought into the movement.[150] The new recruits were able in turn to earn money by introducing individuals from their own social network with their original recruiters. The movement's second source of income was the large quantity of KKK clothing and accessories which were offered to members and non-members, including flags, knives, swords and even "Klan waters."[151] The growing financial success allowed the network of recruiters to expand, providing luxury lifestyles to the KKK leadership. The KKK purchased what was referred to as an Imperial Mansion for Simmons for $200,000; other Grand Dragons were also heavily compensated.[152]

However, the lifestyle of Simmons and his closest companions ultimately met with growing criticism within the movement, eventually leading to leadership transition and to the appointment of Hiram Evans[153] as Simmons' successor in 1922. But the damage had already been done: a combination of popular disdain regarding the corrupt and immoral nature and exploitative behavior of the KKK leadership, internal conflicts, federal investigations, public criticism towards *Klan* relations with neo-Nazi groups and

---

[149] Ku Klux Klan, *Constitution and Laws of the Knights of the Ku Klux Klan (Inc.)*, (Atlanta Georgia: Knights of the Ku Klux Klan, 1921) Article VI, http://archive.lib.msu.edu/DMC/AmRad/constitutionlawsknights.pdf (accessed 3 November 2012).

[150] Quarles (1999), 57.

[151] For example, the standard uniform cost approximately $5, and a robe $12: see Rice, 19.

[152] Katz, 79.

[153] Evans was a dentist from Dallas, Texas; his charismatic personality and educational background facilitated his rise through the organizational ranks of the KKK since joining in 1920. Even more than Forrest, he promoted the militant nature of the KKK: see e.g., his speech shortly after becoming Grand Dragon: "We are armed and equipped; we are ready for any duty…it is true we have already fought some battles, and won some, but we know that the real war is just starting…" (from Frost, 113).

finally the outbreak of the Great Depression—which made the business model of the movement untenable—culminated in mass departure from the movement, especially its middle class members.[154] The latter development left the organization with only core supporters from the relatively poor Southern agricultural areas. The financial implications were severe and the KKK was forced to liquidate assets, including its Imperial Mansion properties.[155] When in spring 1944 the IRS presented a bill of more than half a million dollars to the KKK, which was on the verge of bankruptcy and claiming fewer than 10,000 paying members, the current Imperial Wizard James Colescott announced his decision to disband the organization. It should be noted, however, that while the incorporated KKK became almost totally dysfunctional, the movement's regional Klans, especially in Georgia, remained active, although they assumed a less public, even secretive, stance.[156]

Notwithstanding its less antagonistic image, since its reestablishment in 1915 few KKK branches excluded violence from their agenda. While there are no reliable sources documenting KKK violent activities between its second birth in 1915 until the end of WWII, different estimations and anecdotal evidence enable a reliable approximation of at least several hundred attacks.[157] The violence was aimed at enhancing the organization's social control over communities by a process of violent retribution, intimidation and consolidation, thereby establishing all-white elections, in which African Americans would be prevented from participating; segregation, by attacking individuals, governmental institutions and commercial bodies that did not ban African Americans from public establishments; and by maintaining anti-communist, anti-Catholic sentiment.[158] Hence, it is not surprising that in 1947 the US Attorney General's Office included the KKK on its list of subversive, totalitarian, fascist and communist organizations.[159]

At the same time, KKK's social control was also achieved by legitimate political means. This was evident especially in the South, where many of the communities' religious,

---

[154] Chalmers, 4.

[155] Quarles (1999), 74.

[156] Ibid., 79–92.

[157] For example, *New York World* reported no less than 152 KKK crimes between 1920 and 1921. See Gitlin, 14–15.

[158] Chalmers, 32–3.

[159] Robert P. Ingalls, *Hoods: The Story of the Ku Klux Klan* (New York: G. P. Putnam's Sons, 1979), 81.

political and social leadership consisted of KKK members or individuals closely affiliated with the organization.[160] Klan members achieved success at a state level, as the examples of David Bibb Graves (Alabama's governor in the 1920s and 1930s) and Walter M. Pierce (Oregon's governor in the 1920s) illustrate.[161]

During the late 1940s there were attempts to rebuild the national framework of the KKK under the charismatic leadership of Samuel Green, Georgia's Grand Dragon.[162] However, this ceased with his sudden death in 1949, and in the first years of the 1950s the movement continued its gradual decline into irrelevancy. Except for a few active cells, the organization was completely dormant until the mid-1950s, when the delicate status quo in the South was challenged by the US Supreme Court rulings in 1954 (against "separate but equal" policies in education) and in 1955 (the requirement of racial integration at the district level of schools). Leveraging feelings of resentment and frustration among much of the Southern population, and later the growing negative sentiment towards the civil rights movement, the KKK reemerged as a significant force focusing on the prevention of integration.[163] Thus, towards the end of the 1950s, the surviving chapters included close to 100,000 members.[164] This led to the renewal of attempts to create organizational frameworks nationwide, among them the *Americans for the Preservation of the White Race* and *United Klan of America (UKA)*. The latter became increasingly influential in the mid-1960s and eventually comprised a Klan-like hierarchical structure with branches in different states, led by its own imperial wizard, Robert Shelton.[165]

Nevertheless, the acknowledged national leadership with power over regional Klans which existed in the first and second instances of the movement was not re-established. This did not prevent the regional Klans from maintaining shared norms, routines and protocols. In most Southern states there was a statewide organizational framework

---

[160] Gitlin, 28.

[161] Leonard Weinberg, Ami Pedahzur and Arie Perliger, *Political Parties and Terrorist Groups* (London and New York: Routledge, 2008) (second edition), 70–71.

[162] Quarles (1999), 81–2.

[163] See relevant theoretical discussion on the dynamic between social movements and counter movements in David S. Meyer and Suzanne Staggenborg, "Movements, Countermovements, and the Structure of Political Opportunity," *The American Journal of Sociology*, 101(6) (1996), 1628–60.

[164] Rice, 118.

[165] Some have indicated that in its heyday the *United Klan of America (UKA)* comprised almost 97% of the Klan members in the United States; the North Carolina Klan alone included almost 200 Klaverns and close to 7500 members: see Gitlin, 86.

divided into Klaverns which included between ten and forty members.[166] Transferring between Klaverns was only permitted with permission from both Klavern, and attending other Klaverns' meetings was not allowed without special authorization. Rules and protocols existed for most aspects of the Klaverns' activities including clothing stipulations, admission requirements, Klan ceremony rituals and in-group hierarchy; most Klans continued to use the same terminology for designated ranks, e.g., Imperial Wizard, Dragon, etc.[167]

During the 1950s and 1960s most of the KKK chapters were involved in innumerable violent activities against African Americans and integration supporters, civil rights activists and Jews. These included murder, arson, and the bombing of public facilities and Jewish and Catholic churches.[168] The violence increased between 1956 and 1958, and again between 1963 and 1966, with hundreds of attacks per year and close to 50 complex annual operations, such as bombings and coordinated shooting attacks.[169] There is substantial evidence regarding close cooperation between the KKK and local law enforcement agencies, ranging from turning a blind eye to taking an active role in Klan crimes.[170] Hence, federal agencies, particularly the FBI, were forced to intensify their efforts to contain KKK violence. The FBI was aided by exposure and criticism of the brutal violence of many Klansmen in the burgeoning new media of television, and in the success of the Civil Rights Movement and the growing involvement of the United States in foreign conflicts, which shifted the public mindset from local issues to external threats. Such national changes in technology and in foreign and domestic policy led to a gradual decline in the KKK's violence and membership towards the end of the 1960s. Most estimations indicate that by the early 1970s the KKK consisted of no more than a few thousand members.[171]

But the cyclical nature of the organization's popularity was manifested again in the second half of the 1970s and in the early 1980s as the movement experienced another

---

[166] Quarles (1999), 99–101.

[167] Ibid.

[168] Christopher Hewitt, *Political Violence and Terrorism in Modern America: a Chronology* (Westport, Connecticut: Praeger, 2005).

[169] Ibid.

[170] US Congress, *House Un-American Activities Committee Report on the Activities of the Ku Klux Klan* (Washington, DC: Government Printing Office, 1967), 73.

[171] An ADL report from 1973 argues that the number of KKK members was as low as 5000: see ADL (1973), 12, 87.

upsurge in membership with the appearance of what some scholars designated as the "New Klan" (or the "Klean Klan").[172] The organization now exhibited several new characteristics, among them:[173] (1) the emergence of a new cadre of leaders, more charismatic and communications-savvy than in the past, including college graduates interested in mainstreaming the KKK into legitimate politics (some of them also ran for political positions such as Metzger and Duke); (2) the attempt to attract educated, urban-based activists from the mid and high level socio-demographic echelons; (3) a move toward engaging in publicly visible events and to reducing the level of secrecy (including extensive use of the mainstream media and the newly evolved internet); and lastly, (4) the tendency of a significant minority of KKK leaders to adopt liberal rhetoric which focuses on the need to protect the rights of white people, rather than on assuming social control over other ethnic and religious groups.[174] Many of these leaders, such as David Duke, Louis Beam, Thomas Metzger, Donald Black and Bill Wilkinson were able to expand their Klan significantly, and became familiar figures nationwide. Some also exploited their substantial popularity and publicity in order to establish their own independent white supremacy groups, free from the shadows and constraints of the KKK's traditions and problematic violent image: for example, Tom Metzger established the WAR and David Duke the NAAWP.[175] These new organizations were also a symptom of the growing fragmentation of the movement, and of the attempt to break its boundaries to increase mobilization and cooperation with other far-right groups outside the KKK realm. In the mid to late 1980s, for example, neo-Nazi Skinhead groups in California cooperated with, and were guided by, Metzger's *California Knights* and later WAR.[176] During this period KKK leaders forged close ties with Christian Identity groups such as the *Criminal Extremist Coalition (CEC)* and the *Aryan Nations*.[177] These changes indicate that the KKK was not only experiencing an ideological face-lift, but had also adopted cooperative practices that helped it to gain access to ideologically related movements distinct from the KKK.

The leaders of the new Klan held different perspectives regarding the importance and effectiveness of violence for enhancing the popularity and influence of the movement

---

[172] Gitlin, 36.

[173] Southern Poverty Law Center Klanwatch Staff, 45.

[174] Wyn Craig Wade, 368; NAAWP, 6.

[175] Dobratz and Shanks-Meile, 48–9.

[176] Southern Poverty Law Center Intelligence Project, 17–18.

[177] Quarles (1999), 118–122.

and its values. Whereas David Duke usually rejected the use of violence, others, such as Thomas Metzger, Bill Wilkinson and Louis Beam, continue to support and to emphasize the importance of militant activism. Thus, Metzger established the *Border Watch*, a militia group which patrolled the Mexican border with California and other southern states,[178] and Wilkinson and Beam founded military camps in their Klan territories.[179] Beam was also one of the first to introduce the concept of "leaderless resistance," based on the idea of abandoning the attempts to create a nation-wide hierarchal KKK organization and instead form a leaderless organization consisting of small cells of 6-8 individuals which would operate independently and thus maintain relative immunity to external infiltration and to legislative and administrative counter-terrorism measures.[180] While it is not completely clear whether this was more an intellectual reflection of the then current fragmentation of the KKK and the emergence of groups such as *The Order,* or an attempt to further encourage and strengthen the increasingly cellular nature of the KKK, it is clear that Beam, the *Texas Klan* leader, believed that this was the most efficient structure in response to the strategies employed by the FBI against American far-right groups.[181] Other leaders joined him in advocating leaderless resistance, especially following successful operations against their own organizations, like Thomas Metzger did after the WAR collapsed in the early 1990s.[182]

These different approaches to violent activities reflect a tension between two mobilization tactics. While Duke believed that the future survival of the movement depended on its ability to mobilize support from the more centralized conservative audience, emphasizing the clean and new intellectual nature of the Klan, other leaders such as Beam and Wilkinson believed that the mobilization potential of the movement existed among those who were looking for channels to actively manifest their frustration and resentment towards minorities and the government: their investment in the creation of military-like recruiting and training camps served exactly that aim. This also explains their recruitment efforts among military veterans.

---

[178] Hamm, 44. [179] Lisa Klobuchar, *Birmingham Church Bombing: The Ku Klux Klan's History of Terror* (Mankato, MN: Compass, 1963), 80.

[179] Lisa Klobuchar, *Birmingham Church Bombing: The Ku Klux Klan's History of Terror* (Mankato, MN: Compass, 1963), 80.

[180] Southern Poverty Law Center Klanwatch Staff, 45.

[181] Stephen E. Atkins, *Encyclopedia of Right-Wing Extremism in Modern American History* (New York: ABC-CLIO, 2011), 222–3.

[182] Gitlin, 100.

In the late 1980s and early 1990s the political and public environment again became hostile to the KKK. Several factors contributed to this change in the social and political climate. First was the flourishing of the conservative right under the Reagan Administration and its transformation into a powerful political force, when "mainstream culture [became] anchored with conservatism and family values...that were at the heart of a growing religious revival waged by the fundamentalist Christian right."[183] Thus, the number of conservative Americans who felt disenfranchised and sought radical political alternatives had decreased. Second was the effective use of civilian law suits by civil rights organizations such as the Anti-Defamation League (ADL), the Southern Poverty Law Center (SPLC), and others. Wilkinson's *Louisiana Knights*, for example, eventually collapsed after they were unable to deal with the growing torrent of civil lawsuits; the same process led to the collapse of Robert Shelton's *UKA*.[184] Third, the growing competition with other groups with similar extremist ideological tenets and fewer image problems, such as the militias, the Christian Identity groups, and the Skinheads, added to the difficulty of maintaining the organization's relevance. Finally, while the 1995 Oklahoma CIty bombing directed most of the attention of law enforcement authorities to the militia movement, the KKK also suffered from official scrutiny and public backlash. Hence, in the mid-1990s most assessments indicated that KKK membership was less than 10,000 members nationwide.[185] There are no significant indications that, since then, the KKK has been able to return to its former peak membership numbers, and in many ways it has continued to be overshadowed by its competition.

3.2.1.2 – The American National Socialist Movement and Neo-Nazi Groups

National Socialism has maintained a presence in the American political and social arena since the early 1930s. But unlike other components of the far right, it was never able to transform into a mass movement or gain any access, even limited, to legitimate politics. While some of the theoretical approaches in the political violence literature predict that this leads to further radicalization and provides greater incentive to engage in violence, neo-Nazi organizations' involvement in violence was mostly marginal, at least until the

---

[183] Hamm, 46.
[184] Gitlin, 89.
[185] See for example KKK profile at the SPLC website –
http://www.splcenter.org/get-informed/intelligence-files/ideology/ku-klux-klan.

late 1970s and early 1980s, when new and more militant neo-Nazi groups began to emerge and to cooperate with other far-right groups.

Probably the first significant organized manifestation of support for Nazi ideology in the United States was the Chicago-based *Friends of the New Germany (FOTNG)* which was formed in 1930 as a social organization linking Americans of German origin who identified with the new rising German National-Socialist party.[186] As the latter gained political dominance in Germany, *FOTNG*'s popularity increased, and in the mid-1930s consisted of between 10,000 and 20,000 members, most of them first or second generation German immigrants from Chicago or New York City.[187] In 1936, the *FOTNG* transformed officially into the *German-American Bund*, and under the leadership of Fritz Kuhn (WWI German Army veteran and member of the Nazi Party) focused mainly on spreading anti-Semitic, anti-Communist and anti-Liberal propaganda. This was conducted mainly at rallies and demonstrations, as well as at recreational-indoctrination camps in New York and New Jersey for members and supporters.[188] The *Bund* also created its own version of *Hitler Youth*, aimed at preserving and enhancing the familiarity of future generations of German-Americans with German heritage and culture.[189]

However, despite these attempts to expand the organization's size and influence, the *Bund* never gained momentum. Several causative factors are relevant. To begin with, it failed to convince the Third Reich's leadership to support it financially or ideologically. Moreover, the Nazi regime, understanding that the *Bund's* actions intensified anti-German sentiments in the United States, consistently refused to allow German citizens to join the *Bund* and condemned the use of Nazi emblems and symbols by its members.[190] The German ambassador described *Bund* activities as "stupid and noisy activities."[191] Second, Kuhn himself, with his poor English and limited understanding of American culture, was rarely able to relate to German-Americans and was a major burden for an organization looking to gain sympathy within the American-German

---

[186] Remak, 38–41.

[187] Dobratz and Shanks-Meile, 55–7.

[188] Canedy, 190–91.

[189] For more on the Bund see Leland Bell, "The Failure of Nazism in America," *Political Science Quarterly*, 85(4) (1970), 585-599; Gene Smith, "Bundesfuehrer Kuhn," *American Heritage* 46(5) (1995), 102.

[190] Bell.

[191] Ibid.

public. Finally, as the United States became more involved in the war, there was a growing perception in the law enforcement community that the *Bund* harbored subversive potential. This led to a series of federal and local investigations against the organization, and to its eventual dissolution in December 1941.[192]

While the Second World War witnessed the defeat of Nazi Germany, the Nazi ideology never entirely disappeared from the political realms in the West, nor did it do so in Europe, which experienced the emergence of far-right fascist parties shortly after the end of the war. Nor did it vanish in the United States, where several highly centralized neo-Nazi groups raised their heads in the 1950s and 1960s. The first among these was the *National Renaissance Party* (NRP), established in 1949 by James Madole. This cult-like organization, which ceased to exist after the death of Madole in 1978, focused principally on conducting public rallies and demonstrations and producing National-Socialist propaganda via the "National Renaissance Bulletin." It promoted ideas regarding the need to free the entertainment and media industries from Jewish control.[193] Although the NRP formed its own elite guard, which was mostly used for protecting Madole from angry protesters during NRP rallies, there are no indications of the involvement of the party in violent activities, or that it was able to garner support beyond its core of several dozen supporters in New York State.[194]

A decade after the NRP was formed it was joined by *The American Nazi Party* (ANP),[195] an organization that would become not just the face of American neo-Nazism in the 1960s, but also a breeding ground for the leaders of American neo-Nazism in the following decades. The ANP was founded by George Lincoln Rockwell, former WWII Navy veteran, and a charismatic and skilled speaker who understood the power of the rising mass media in drawing attention to his ideas and to ANP activities.[196] As in the NRP, ANP activities were mainly comprised of rallies, demonstrations, public speaking events and the publication of ANP propaganda. The propaganda was disseminated via two bulletins: "The Stormtrooper" and the "Rockwell Report," which were aimed at

---

[192] Canedy, 224–5.

[193] John George and Laird Wilcox, *Nazis, Communists, Klansman and others on the Fringe* (Buffalo, New York: Prometheus Books, 1992), 352–4.

[194] Hewitt.

[195] Initially the organization was named the "World Union of Free Enterprise National Socialists" (WUFENS), but Rockwell and the media quickly started to refer to it as the ANP: see FBI file, 11.

[196] For comprehensive documentation of ANP activities, see Schmaltz.

exposing the cooperation between American Jewry and communists, and advancing ideas of racial segregation.[197] The NRP and ANP also shared a similar organizational structure. The ANP had a highly centralized structure, in which "Commander" Rockwell was the only meaningful authority. Understandably, the NRP headquarters in Arlington, Virginia—the base of the "Stormtrooper" rank-and-file members, which was also known as "Hatemonger Hill"—was managed as a military base under the leadership of Rockwell.[198] The members were divided by rank, wore uniforms, and subjected to strict discipline. Moreover, all new members participated in three days of ideological training, which concluded with a commencement ceremony.[199]

Rockwell was able to attract significant attention via the ANP's endless inflammatory events and initiatives.[200] He publicized its legal struggles against those who tried to prevent him from disseminating ANP materials and conducting party events in public areas. The ANP was able to establish several branches outside Virginia (*Fighting American Nationalists* groups were formed in Chicago, New York City, Pennsylvania, Ohio, Maryland, California, Dallas and Illinois; and some branches of the ANP youth movement, *White Youth Corps*, were established in California, Chicago, Washington DC and New York City).[201] However, most indications are that the party was never able to grow beyond a few hundred members.[202] This was also reflected in the complete failure of Rockwell's campaign for the governorship of Virginia during 1965 in which he garnered less than one percent of the vote.[203] The campaign nonetheless displayed the conviction of Rockwell and his followers that the party's road to power would be through non-violent political means, a path that was also articulated in the ANP political program.[204]

The ANP failed to generate stable sources of income, most of the time relying on membership fees of $5 per month, and a onetime $10 initiation fee, and small donations

---

[197] FBI file on ANP, 18–30.

[198] FBI file on ANP, 37–45.

[199] FBI file on ANP, 44.

[200] See e.g., Rockwell's "hate bus" initiative. During 1961, as a response to *CORE's (Congress of National Equality)* "Freedom Ride," Rockwell organized a cross-country trip for 12 ANP members from DC to New Orleans, on a Volkswagen bus, to protest against "Race Mixing": see also Schmaltz, 116-117.

[201] Schmaltz, 39, 57.

[202] According to the relevant FBI files, the number never exceeded 100.

[203] Schmaltz, 247–9.

[204] Ibid.

from relatively affluent sympathizers.[205] This is not surprising, since most indications suggest that the majority of ANP members and supporters were usually from low socio-economic echelons, and a relatively large number had criminal records.[206]

In view of the mobilization and funding challenges presented above, Rockwell concluded that the association with Nazi Germany was the main obstacle in mobilizing support for the ANP. More specifically, even though many white Americans identified with the principles of National Socialism, the foreign, Nazi image of the party deterred them from seriously considering joining or supporting it. Thus, in January 1967 Rockwell changed the party name to *National Socialist White People's Party* (NSWPP) and changed its slogan from "Sieg Heil" to "White Power." He issued the party's ten point program, which emphasized the need to fight for all-white America and to eradicate the control of American Jewry over American culture, finance and politics.[207] Nonetheless, organizationally and operationally the ANP did not experience any significant changes. Such drastic organizational change only occurred with the assassination of Rockwell in August 1967 by John Palter, a former ANP member who had been expelled from the party by Rockwell several months earlier.[208]

The death of Rockwell, particularly the absence of a natural and consensual successor, led many prominent members of the ANP to depart and form their own organizations, among them the *National Socialist Party of America* (NSPA), led by Frank Colin, the *White Party of America*, led by Karl Helen, the *National White People*, led by Charles White, and perhaps most importantly, the *National Alliance*, founded by William Pierce in 1970.[209] The ANP, suffering from the exodus of prominent members, and without its charismatic leader, experienced a long decline in terms of membership and public influence. Branches in many major cities were shut down, such as in Los Angeles and Chicago, the barracks were abandoned and the headquarters were eventually relocated to Milwaukee.[210] In 1984 Matt Koehl, Rockwell's successor, decided to restructure the party ideology by adding religious and Christian Identity components and adopting structures and norms similar to those of a cult. He claimed that Hitler was the gift of an

---

[205] FBI file on ANP, 49–50.

[206] FBI file on the ANP, 33.

[207] Schmaltz, 304–5.

[208] Ibid., 320–23.

[209] George and Wilcox, 363–5.

[210] In 1983 they moved to a suburb of Milwaukee (New Berlin). See George and Wilcox, 359.

inscrutable divine providence, sent to rescue the white race from decadence and extinction.[211] In this context, he announced that the party would be renamed *New Order*.[212] These changes had limited effect, however, as the party found it difficult to expand beyond its several dozen members and close to a hundred supporters. Today, the name *American Nazi Party* has been adopted by a group run by Rocky J. Suhayda, a former member of Rockwell's original ANP. Based in Westland, Michigan, Suhayda's ANP website sells nostalgic reprints of Rockwell's 1960s-era magazine "The Stormtrooper," and holds semi-private annual meetings in Laurens, South Carolina.[213]

To conclude, the inability of the ANP to mobilize significant support was a result of several factors, including its reliance for many years on foreign National Socialist heritage and jargon; a rigid ideological framework which made the party less competitive in the far-right universe; the military culture of the party, which intimidated many potential supporters; the avoidance of violent/action-oriented initiatives, which alienated those seeking a militant framework; and finally, the limited funds available to sustain party operations.

As mentioned above, the vacuum left by the decline of the ANP was filled by organizations led by Rockwell's former followers, and by groups such as *the National Socialist Movement, National Socialist Vanguard, Nationalist Socialist White American Party, National Socialist League*, and *Euro-American Alliance*.[214] Hence, the decline of the ANP facilitated the breakdown of American national socialism from a relatively cohesive framework in the late 1950s and early 1960s into an accumulation of smaller fragments, many of these consisting of only a handful of members and with no operational or political capabilities. As a consequence, these small groups focused mainly on the distribution of neo-Nazi literature.[215] The limited capabilities of the groups were also a result of their reluctance to engage cooperatively with each other. Considering the limited cadre each one of these groups possessed, the leaders of the different groups were careful when engaging in joint operations, fearing that this would enhance

---

[211] For more information on the ideological tenets of the New Order see - http://theneworder.org/reading/
[212] In 1988 the ADL estimated the *New Order*'s number of members to be approximately 100: see ADL (1988) *Hate Groups*, 49.
[213] http://www.americannaziparty.com/
[214] George and Wilcox, 364–8.
[215] Dobratz and Shanks-Meile, 59–63.

defections.[216] Defections were a common feature within the movement during the 1970s and 1980s. Moreover, it seems that the strong competitive nature of most of the leaders further discouraged cooperation.

Perhaps the most important effect of the fragmentation process, especially in the context of this study, is the growing tendency of neo-Nazis to engage in violence, something which was very rare if not absent under Rockwell's leadership. For example, NSPA members were involved in a shootout with members of the Communist Workers Party in 1979 during an event the media titled "The Greensboro Massacre."[217] In another incident in 1980, *National Socialist Liberation Front* members were involved in a shooting of African Americans at Metairie, Louisiana.[218] Similarly, *SS Action Group* (SSAG) members were frequently involved in violent confrontations with members of different liberal and left-wing organizations.[219] The growing competition within the far-right National Socialist arena, as well as the gradual fading of Rockwell's legacy of nonviolent practices, contributed to this trend.

Finally, another recent trend among neo-Nazi groups is the growing cooperation with groups outside the realm of neo-Nazism. In the post-Rockwell era, many groups increasingly assumed a more pluralistic nature, avoiding restriction of their ideology to National Socialism and willingly merging it with similar neighboring ideological creeds. For example, both the *Social Nationalist Aryan Peoples' Party* and the *National Socialist Liberation Front* were highly populated by, and cooperated with local KKK members and associations.[220] The opposite was also the case, as some of the new and existing white supremacy and Christian Identity groups started to adopt National Socialist concepts. Perhaps the most glaring example is the *Aryan Nations*: although it

---

[216] George and Wilcox, 360–8.

[217] Greensboro Truth and Reconciliation Commission Report, Executive Summary (25 May 2006), http://www.greensborotrc.org/exec_summary.pdf (accessed 3 November 2012).

[218] George and Wilcox, 364–5.

[219] Ibid., 367–8.

[220] See e.g., Matt Koehl, *NS Bulletin* (November, 1982), "In the past, the New Order/NSWPP has been very hesitant to hold joint activities with other racialist organizations. But, as part of our new outreach, we felt that this occasion would be the perfect one in which not merely to give lip-service to White Unity, but rather to give a practical demonstration of it".

was formed as a Christian Identity organization, it increasingly absorbed significant National Socialist elements.[221]

The two trends, of increasing propensity toward violence and cooperation with other far-right organizations have further intensified in the past two decades, and will be discussed more fully in the empirical section of this study.

3.2.1.3 – Skinheads

While for analytical reasons the Skinheads have been analyzed in this study as a separate far-right stream, many researchers tend to frame them as a modern, younger extension of American National Socialism.[222] Indeed, Skinhead groups share several similarities with American neo-Nazi groups. Its members display a fascination with Nazi symbols, regalia and terminology, and like the neo-Nazi groups, they are also an American extension of a socio-political phenomenon which emerged initially in Europe (in this case, the UK). The first reports of the appearance of Skinheads in the streets of urban America occurred in the early 1980s in the Midwest and Texas.[223] There is no evidence, however, of any significant organizational framework or of systematic violence produced by the early Skinhead associations, which mostly could be described as small and relatively unorganized social networks of youths who embraced European Skinhead subculture and punk music.[224] White supremacy ideology still exerted a relatively marginal influence on the American Skinhead subculture at that time. It is therefore not surprising that in some areas nonracist Skinhead groups included members of minority groups, often African American and Hispanic.[225]

A division within the American Skinhead scene occurred towards the mid to late 1980s, as some of the Skinhead groups began to absorb white supremacy ideology, engaging in violent activities with racist characteristics and forging relations with other far-right organizations. In the Chicago area in late 1984, for example, influenced by Hitler's *Mein Kampf* and exposed to British white power punk music, Clark Reid Martell and twelve

---

[221] See relevant sections of this study, and FBI file *Aryan Nation*, Parts 1 and 2, http://vault.fbi.gov/Aryan%20Nation (accessed 3 November 2012).

[222] While most academics and practitioners acknowledge the differences between the traditional American neo-Nazi movement and the Skinheads subculture, my impression is that the sub-text in many publications depicts the latter as a youthful extension of the first.

[223] Southern Poverty Law Center Intelligence Project, 4.

[224] Hamm, 37.

[225] Ibid.

of his close friends established a group called *Romantic Violence*, which would later be named CASH: *Chicago Area Skinheads*.[226] In the following months, *Romantic Violence* became involved in a series of violent incidents perpetrated against Hispanic and Jewish victims, and it worked with the local cell of the ANP in spreading racist propaganda and white power music.[227]

On the West Coast, similar dynamics could be observed. In 1985 the *American Front* was established in the San Francisco area by Robert Heick who, with several companions, distributed white power punk music and propaganda and engaged in severe attacks against interracial couples, Jews and other minorities.[228] While the local police took action against *American Front*, the new propaganda force *White Aryan Resistance* expanded the presence of neo-Nazi Skinheads on the West Coast and eventually helped to develop the new movement in other parts of the country.

Starting in 1986, hundreds of Skinheads were mobilized to adopt white-supremacy ideology via organized outreach propaganda operations of the *White Aryan Resistance* (WAR), which was founded and led by Thomas Metzger after he left the KKK.[229] The outreach operations included: forging connections with dominant figures from the European Skinheads and white power music scene and introducing them via WAR to American Skinhead groups;[230] the production and distribution of a youth magazine named the WAR Zine, which combined National Socialist and white supremacy messages with reports and news from the white power music scene;[231] the broadcasting and distribution of "Race and Reason" white supremacy propaganda videotapes which featured speeches by Metzger and other prominent WAR members;[232] frequent appearances on nationally syndicated television shows presenting the fundamentals of the Skinhead culture; the creation and management of an electronic bulletin board known as the WAR board, and hotline services with information about WAR and

---

[226] John Leo, "A Chilling Wave of Racism," *Time,* January (25) (1988), 57; ADL, (1988), *Hate Groups*; ADL, *Young and Violent: The Growing Menace of America's Neo Nazi Skinheads* (New York: ADL, 1988).
[227] See ADL, *Shaved for Battle: Skinheads Target America's Youth* (New York: ADL publications, 1987), 3.
[228] ADL, (1988) *Young and Violent*; Coplon, 87.
[229] Southern Poverty Law Center Intelligence Project, 17–18.
[230] Ibid.
[231] Hamm, 52.
[232] Owen Brown, "Know your Enemy…Tom Metzger and the American Fascist," *No KKK! No Facist USA!* Spring/Summer (1989), 5–6; Bill Wallace, "Racist Group Using Computers and TV to Recruit in Bay Area," *SF Chronicle*, 5 March (1985), 1–2.

Skinhead activities.[233] Finally, Metzger intensified WAR presence in colleges via collaboration with the *Aryan Youth Movement* (AYM), which had roots in a number of academic institutions, and through nationwide tours which also helped to establish ties with local Skinheads in other parts of the country.[234]

The implications of the Skinhead shift towards the fringes of the American far right were quickly visible. During the late 1980s, Skinheads were involved in several hundred violent attacks and acts of vandalism against non-Aryan facilities such as Jewish stores and synagogues, and against homosexuals and other minorities.[235] While a large part of the Skinhead ideology focused on the need to defeat what they believed to be Jewish-controlled governmental institutions, Skinheads' attacks were usually aimed at different representations of out-groups, such as minorities and people with alternative lifestyles, and were rarely if ever directed against governmental targets.[236] Moreover, while many of the Skinhead groups' social activities enjoyed a high level of coordination and preplanning, their violent attacks were typically opportunistic. Skinheads would typically refer to their assaults as fights, implying spontaneous incidents, and framed them in the context of self-defense. For example, in his study of the Skinheads subculture of the 1980s and early 1990s, Hamm (1993) was unable to identify one Skinhead interviewee who admitted that he was involved in a preplanned violent incident.[237] In any case, the massive wave of violence which accompanied the growth of the American Skinhead subculture—available reports estimate that the number of racist Skinheads grew between 1987 and 1990 from several hundred to between four and five thousand—led the US Attorney General in 1989 to emphasize the American government commitment to spare no effort in order to counter the "…shocking reemergence of hate group violence."[238] Indeed, the late 1980s and early 1990s witnessed growing efforts by federal law enforcement agencies and the political arena to counter the Skinhead subculture, including implementation of the "Hate Crime Statistics Act."[239] In addition, nonracist Skinheads contributed to this struggle, as in

---

[233] Peter Stills, "Dark Contagion: Bigotry and Violence Online," *PC Computing*, December (1989), 144–9.
[234] Hamm, 57.
[235] William Tafoya, *Rioting in the Street: Déjà vu*, Address before the Office of International Criminal Justice, Chicago (1990).
[236] Hamm, 74.
[237] Hamm, 154.
[238] Paul M. Barrett, "Hate Crimes Increase and Become More Violent: US Prosecutors Focus on Skinheads Movement," *Wall Street Journal* (1989), A12.
[239] Mary H. Cooper, "The Growing Danger of Hate Groups," *Editorial Research Report*, 18 (1989), 262–75.

many cities they made a significant effort to limit the expansion and recruitment efforts of neo-Nazi Skinheads.[240]

Organizationally, anthropological and sociological studies of the neo-Nazi Skinhead subculture suggest that while some of the early neo-Nazi Skinhead groups exhibited a flat network structure with limited hierarchy and institutionalization, several of the WAR-associated Skinhead groups (WAR *Skin*) did assume a paramilitary structure. These groups employed military ranks, held roster sheets and a report/activities card on each of their members. Apparently, these were used for assessing suitability for advancement. Some of the groups possessed tangible assets such as headquarters and living quarters for their members.[241] It is also important to note that despite WAR propaganda efforts, recruitment remained mainly based on secondary social ties and differential association.[242]

WAR attempts to create a nationwide organization of neo-Nazi Skinheads stumbled, mainly as a result of the collapse of WAR in the late 1980s.[243] An alternative emerged from the South which would eventually succeed in forming a nationwide white supremacist Skinhead organizational framework; the *Hammerskin Nations* (also known as the *Hammerskins* or HSN) arose from the *Confederate Hammerskins* (CHS) which had begun to consolidate in Dallas between 1985 and 1987.[244] This group was not merely one of the more violent Skinhead groups at that time, but was also highly efficient at publicizing its activities, engaging in successful recruitment from among the developed nonracist Skinhead scene in the Dallas area, as well as being relatively well funded.[245] While these factors facilitated the quick expansion of the group in the Dallas area, how

---

[240] Jack B. Moore, *Skinheads Shaved For Battle: A Cultural History of American Skinheads* (Madison, Wisconsin: Bowling Green University Press, 1993), 138

[241] Floyd Clarke, "Hate Violence in the United States," *FBI Bulletin*, January (1991), 14–17.

[242] T. J. Leyden and Bridget M. Cook, *Skinhead Confessions: From Hate to Hope* (Springville, Utah: Sweetwater, 2008), 91–8. The concept of differential association, originally developed by Edwin Sutherland to explain engagement in criminal activity, emphasizes the role of social interactions in the learning and internalization of values, attitudes and motives.

[243] Southern Poverty Law Center Intelligence Project, 18.

[244] ADL, "Extremism in America: the Hammerskin Nation," *Anti-Defamation League*, http://www.adl.org/learn/ext_us/hammerskin.asp (accessed 3 November 2012); HSN, "Who We Are…/ Our History…," *Hammerskin Nation*, http://www.hammerskins.net/ (accessed 3 November 2012).

[245] Pete Simi and Barbara Brents, "An Extreme Response to Globalization: The Case of Racist Skinheads," in ed. Michael Flynn and David C. Brotherton, *Globalizing the Streets* (New York: Columbia University Press, 2008), 195–6.

can we explain its nationwide expansion? Several factors may help explain the transformation of the group into a nation-wide organization.

First, already at the early stages of the consolidation of the CHS, its leaders were conscious of their aspiration to find a way to unite the regional manifestations of neo-Nazi Skinheads. Thus, prominent members of CHS actively began to attend events of similar groups all over the country and to promote cooperation; indeed, many of these groups would eventually become HSN branches during 1988 and 1989, especially in Oklahoma, Tennessee and in other Texas cities.[246] Secondly, the CHS was effective in using large-scale regional cultural events organized by far-right associations to attract new groups to join the HSN organizational umbrella. In 1988, for example, SKINFEST in Milwaukie led to several major Skinhead groups from Wisconsin joining the emerging HSN.[247] Similarly, the Aryan Fest in Oklahoma the same year provided significant momentum for the recruitment of Southern-based groups; and the Aryan Woodstock in California planted the seeds for the emergence of HSN teams in Southern California.[248] Finally, interpersonal relations and the migration of CHS members to other parts of the country also assisted in forging ties with new groups and persuading them to join the organizational umbrella of the HSN: cases in point are groups in Maine, Northern California and Chicago, which joined the HSN during 1989.[249]

During the late 1980s and early 1990s the HSN continued to grow at a fast pace. After the formal establishment in 1988 of the Northern chapter of the HSN (NHS), similar regional branches formed in the following years in other areas, and in the mid-1990s the HSN already included more than 30 branches throughout the United States, which were organized in several regional groupings including the *Western Hammerskin* (WSN), *Rocky Mountain Hammerskin* (RHS) and *Eastern Hammerskin* (EHS).[250] In 1994, when the *Hammerskin Nations* was formally established, the organization also looked outside the United States, forming relations with European Skinheads, initially with groups in Switzerland and Northern Ireland, but later also with groups from other European countries, mostly in Western Europe, e.g., Germany, Spain, Italy.[251]

---

[246] Ibid; see also HSN, "Who We Are…/ Our History…"

[247] Ibid.

[248] Ibid.

[249] Ibid and ADL, "Extremism in America: the Hammerskin Nation".

[250] Simi and Brents, 195–6; see also HSN, "Who We Are…/ Our History…"

[251] Ibid.

While the mid to late 1990s saw further HSN international branches formed in Canada, Australia and New Zealand, these years were also characterized by the emergence of internal conflicts within the organization. These were associated with two main issues. The first was the balance of power between the local branches and the national leadership. While the formal establishment of the HSN in 1994 represented an attempt to create a national leadership, based in Dallas, with significant power over the local branches, the counter-response of those opposing the elitist tendencies of the HSN top rank officers led to defections of several regional branches, mainly in Indiana and Ohio: these included the *Outlaw Hammerskins* and *Hoosier State Skinheads*.[252] More specifically, the HSN leadership, interested in transforming the Skinheads into the elite force of the White Supremacy American movement, introduced a strict recruitment procedure for those interested in joining the organization, and codes of conduct, including restrictions on violent behavior.[253] A growing number of members manifested their frustration at the institutionalization of the Skinhead subculture by deserting and forming new kinds of Skinhead groups, even more violent, less reluctant to engage in criminal activities and with the tendency to absorb elements of the African-American street gang subculture (in many Skinheads circles they were designated simply as *Outlaw Hammerskin*).[254]

The emergence of these new Skinhead groups also reflected a generational gap within the movement. As the original HSN leadership entered mid-life, their ability to relate to the new generation of Skinheads dwindled and a growing ideological and mental gap became evident. This led to a decline in the number of members and new recruits, and an increase in doubts about the commitment of the HSN leadership to militant activism.[255] An attempt to downgrade the severity of these concerns led the HSN leadership in 1999 and 2000 to provide more freedom and flexibility to the local chapters as well as reshaping the borders between the different regional organizations, including the creation of a new branch, the Midlands Hammerskins (MHS).[256] The effectiveness of these steps was limited, as the Skinhead scene continued its fragmentation, and rising numbers of groups distanced themselves from the HSN.

---

[252] Southern Poverty Law Center Intelligence Project, 12–13.
[253] Ibid.
[254] Southern Poverty Law Center Intelligence Project, 5.
[255] Ibid.
[256] HSN, "Who We Are…/ Our History…"

Current trends within the Skinhead scene, including the current role of the HMS and its involvement in contemporary Skinhead violence, will be analyzed further in the empirical section of the study. Analysis of the development of the Skinhead movement in America would not be complete without addressing its cultural dimension, and in particular the role of white power music. It is not a coincidence that the first Skinhead event on a national level was a white power music festival, organized with the assistance of WAR in 1988.[257] As mentioned in the ideological overview of the Skinhead subculture, the original Skinhead scene emerged from ska, reggae and punk music clubs. The racist Skinheads eventually separated from the mainstream by following a specific branch of punk music dedicated to white supremacy and neo-Nazi messages.[258] The first and the most prominent of the bands comprising this style of punk-rock music was "Skrewdriver." Led by one of the most prominent figures of the European Skinhead movement, Ian Stuart Donaldson, it inspired the formation of similar bands and became in many ways the ideological beacon of the movement. To illustrate, Hamm's study of American Skinheads mentioned earlier could not locate any Skinheads who did not frequently listen to Skrewdriver albums.[259]

In summary, white power music filled three key social roles in the expansion of Skinhead subculture. The first was its function as a tool of mobilization and, more specifically, in inspiring potential recruits with Skinhead attitudes and language. For many would-be Skinheads, white power music was their first encounter with the ideological and cultural foundations of the Skinheads' way of life. Hence, the music served as a catalyst for their further familiarization with the subculture.[260] However, the white power music was much more than a mere mobilization tool; it also became a main instrument for the consolidation of white supremacy ideology as an inherent part of the neo-Nazi Skinhead subculture. In a subculture which for many years was comprised of isolated, informal, and unstable cells, white power music was the unifying medium which enabled the formation of a cohesive ideological framework, including identification of the movement's main adversaries, its fundamental values, norms and practices.[261] In this context, the music also facilitated the emergence of what can be described as the Skinhead "language," which includes shared concepts, terms and

---

[257] Southern Poverty Law Center Intelligence Project, 11.
[258] Simi and Brents, 196–9.
[259] Hamm, 32–5.
[260] Simi and Brents, 196–9.
[261] Ibid.

framing of political and social reality. Moreover, in many cases the music provided operational blueprints for the Skinhead group, especially in terms of legitimizing violent tendencies.[262] Finally, the music was also an instrument used by the movement's elites—and by far-right organizations interested in linking themselves with the Skinheads—to enhance their influence and their control within the Skinhead scene, and to shape its ideological development. Hence, it is no coincidence that HSN, WAR and other associations were engaged in organizing hate rock festivals and concerts, and in forming white power record labels.[263]

3.2.2 – The Militia Movement: Organizational and Operational Evolution

For many years the "militia" concept had enduring and positive roots in the American collective mindset. This was a reflection of the significant role played by civilian paramilitary groups in the American violent struggle for independence, and later in providing security at times of territorial expansion. However, whereas Americans continue to remember and admire the role of militias in the Revolutionary War, i.e., the Minutemen in the battles of Lexington and Concord, growing numbers of scholars, policy makers and practitioners express concern at the modern manifestations of American militias and the threat they represent.

While the social, economic and political conditions served as a basis for the rapid growth of the militia movement during the late 1980s and early 1990s, attempts by the far-right scene to promote paramilitary subcultures could already be witnessed in the 1960s.[264] Catalysts for the formation of the militia movement was Ruby Ridge and Waco incidents, which set off a dynamic which transformed an existing subculture into a

---

[262] Ibid.

[263] Ibid.

[264] The most famous of those is probably the "Minutemen," a Missouri-based group founded by Robert DePugh in 1960 in order to protect America from the Communist threat. For a decade it engaged in paramilitary training and stockpiling of ammunition. While the number of active members reached approximately two thousand at its peak, the group was eventually dissolved in 1970 after DePugh was convicted of violation of gun control legislation. During the 1980s (as mentioned in the section analyzing the KKK operational evolution), several KKK branches engaged in paramilitary activities and in the formation of military-styled camps, e.g., in 1981, a KKK "military camp" was established near Birmingham Alabama. Around the same time the Posse Comitatus, closely linked with the Christian Identity group, started to organize militia training exercises in Kansas. It appears that the idea of forming militia groups was not new within far-right extremist organizations prior to the emergence of the anti-federalist militia movement in the early to mid-1990s.

violent counterculture. [265] Both events were not just responsible for an escalation in the hostile perceptions towards the federal government among people from rural and mid-America, but they also engraved in the minds of the public the understanding that self-defense of their way of life and values, inevitability meant acting against, or vigilantly protecting themselves from, the federal authorities.[266]

The immediate impact of the Ruby Ridge incident was reflected in a meeting that was held at Estes Park, Colorado, when between 23 and 25 October around 160 members and leaders of various American far-right groups convened in order to discuss the appropriate response to, and the implications of what they perceived to be an increasing tendency of the American government to invade segments of the civilian sphere which are supposed to be constitutionally protected.[267] Some resources maintain that at this meeting a consensus was reached that public concern regarding the threat to constitutional rights should be exploited for mobilization and recruitment to the far-right scene.[268] Another consensus consolidated around the need to encourage formation of a loose network of mostly independent militias in accordance with Louis Beam's leaderless resistance doctrine. Beam had participated in the event and that year published his famous manifesto regarding the need of the American far-right to shift to an organizational structure and strategy of leaderless resistance/phantom cells.[269] Also attending the meeting was Larry Pratt, the head of *Gun Owners of America* (GOA). Pratt recommended the creation of units of freedom fighter militias which would fight

---

[265] Movements and groups advocating for the protection of Constitutional rights and diminution of the federal government power were part of the American cultural and political scene long before the emergence of the modern militias in the 1990s: see discussion in this work, see for example Daniel Levitas, *Terrorist Next Door, The Militia Movement and the Radical Right* (New York: St. Martin's press, 2003).

[266] Most texts on the militia movement provide comprehensive descriptions of these events; see e.g., Lane Crothers, *Race on the Right: The American Militia Movement from Ruby Ridge to Homeland Security* (Lanham, Maryland: Rowman & Littlefield, 2003), 75–86.

[267] Snow, 13–14.

[268] Morris Dees, and James Corcoran, *Gathering Storms: The Story of America's Militia Network* (New York: HarperCollins, 1996), 49–67. As with the case of the *Ruby Ridge and Waco* incidents, the Estes Park meeting also became a mythical event in the history of the American far right, analyzed in numerous texts: see Leonard Zeskind, "Armed and Dangerous," *Rolling Stone Magazine,* (November 1995), http://www.rickross.com/reference/militia/militia7.html (accessed 3 November 2012).

[269] The Leaderless Resistance program was published originally by Beam in the 1992 issue of *the Seditionist*: see ADL, "Extremists in America: Louis Beam," *Anti-Defamation League,* http://www.adl.org/learn/ext_us/beam.asp?xpicked=2&item=beam (accessed 3 November 2012); see also Quarles (1999), 147.

against "…communist death squads."[270] In any case, both decisions reflected the understanding of many within the American far right that the Ruby Ridge incident was not an isolated occurrence, but rather a reflection of a growing tension between some parts of the American society and their government, and that the anti-institutional tendencies of most of the potential recruits lent itself to a flat movement with limited hierarchy.

One of the byproducts of the Estes Park meeting was the formation of *United Citizens for Justice* (UCJ), a white supremacy organization which exploited civil rights rhetoric to persuade the government to "return…to a position of service to the people, and the defender of individual rights as our forefathers had intended."[271] Although most of its leaders were members of organizations such as KKK and AN, the organization avoided sliding into the usual racist and nativist agenda and focused mainly on anti-federalist rhetoric. And although the UCJ was in decline by 1994, the idea had taken hold and three of its members founded what is considered the first modern American militia.[272]

The *Montana Militia* (MOM) was established by members of the Trochmann family—the brothers John and David, and David's son, Randy—in early 1994. In contrast to many of the militias that followed, it was engaged mainly in propaganda and public relations initiatives, and much less, if at all, in violent or paramilitary activities.[273] The effective manner in which MOM leadership was able to attract media attention and publicize and disseminate its ideological vision made it an ideological beacon for people with similar views throughout the country. MOM's output included: the journal *Taking Aim* and other highly popular publications such as the *Blue Book*, which was comprised of a binder with media excerpts supposedly confirming New World Order conspiracy theories; special guides for military activities and newsletters; militia accessories and videotapes; and endless public appearances at gun shows, in gun clubs, at survivalist workshops and expos. Some within the militia movement criticized the Trochmanns' avoidance of militant activism. However, they were able to provide a voice, and more

---

[270] See Southern Poverty Law Center, "False Patriots: Profiles of 40 antigovernment leaders: Church as State—Howard Phillips, 60," *Southern Poverty Law Center Intelligence Report*, Summer, 102 (2001), http://www.splcenter.org/get-informed/intelligence-report/browse-all-issues/2001/summer/false-patriots?page=0,8 (accessed 3 November 2012).

[271] See ADL, "Extremists in America: Militia of Montana," *Anti-Defamation League*, http://www.adl.org/learn/ext_us/mom.asp?xpicked=3&item=mom (accessed 3 November 2012).

[272] Snow, 14.

[273] Neil Hamilton, 30–34.

importantly, an inspiration to the many Americans sharing the same frustrations regarding what they perceived as the changing nature of America, and especially the expanding influence and powers of federal authorities.[274]

New militias continued to form during 1994 and 1995. Most of the groups emerged as local initiatives in rural areas, characterized by small and isolated communities and based on dense and relatively small extended family and social networks of white men from the lower and middle levels of society.[275] As in many cases of social networks based on close and long-term social ties and which operate on the fringes of the legal sphere, recruitment was invariably based on previous acquaintanceship rather than on an institutionalized recruitment process which would involve stages of identifying potential recruits, indoctrination and operational training.[276] This facilitated trust between the militia members, ideological cohesion, and made the group more challenging for authorities to infiltrate. When attempts were made to expand the militia beyond the core network of founders, a variety of mechanisms were used to garner recruits, including the introduction of NWO theories and the exploitation of recruits' sentiments concerning topical issues such as the expansion of gun control, environmental legislation, government promotion of liberal social policies, e.g., Clinton's health reform initiative, and the changing demography of American society, particularly through ostensibly xenophilic immigration policies.[277]

Although there are varied estimations of the overall scope of the militia movement at that time, the prevailing view is that in late 1995 the movement was comprised of militias in at least 30 states and included several hundreds of thousands of supporters and active members: some estimations put the number at several million.[278] While there were attempts to create an umbrella organization to unify the movement or at least to create a means of coordination, such as the *Third National Congress*, which convened in

---

274 See ADL, "Extremists in America: Militia of Montana,"; Dees and Corcoran; Beth Hawkins, "Patriot Games," in ed. Dani Hazan, L. Smith, C. Triano, *Militias In America* (San Francisco, California: Institute for Alternative Journalism, 1994), 7–12.

275 For the most up-to-date analysis on geographic distribution of the Militias, see Joshua D. Freilich, *State Level Variations in Militia Activities* (New York: LFB, 2003).

276 See e.g., Ami Pedahzur and Arie Perliger, "The Changing Nature of Suicide Attacks - a Social Network Perspective," *Social Forces*, 84(4) (2006), 1983–2004.

277 See also analysis of the militia movement earlier in this study.

278 Note, however, that some estimations are much lower: Berlet and Lyons provide an assessment of between 15,000 and 40,000: see Chip Berlet and Matthew N. Lyons, "Militia Nation," *The Progressive* 59(6) (1995), 22.

Kansas during October 1996, none of these were successful and the militia movement remained decentralized, with no identifiable national leaders or organizational framework.[279]

While many of the new militias, such as MOM, were careful to stay within legal boundaries and focused mainly on ideological propaganda, e.g., Linda Thompson's *Unorganized Militia of the United States*, other militias assumed a different path. The most well-known of these groups was the *Michigan Militia*. Established by firearm store-owner Norm Olson a few months after the formation of MOM, it assumed a paramilitary organizational structure subordinate to the Militia Corps, headed by MG. Four divisions were created that were administered by COL, and these in turn were divided into brigades commanded by LTC. They conducted military-style training and stockpiled military equipment; raids on militias' compounds in the mid-1990s frequently located dozens to hundreds of firearms and thousands of rounds of ammunition.[280] Stockpiling of equipment was aided by a legal loophole which permitted hobbyists—namely those people convening gun shows—to sell personal firearms without paperwork or waiting periods. This enabled militia members to acquire multiple firearms with minimal bureaucratic obstacles.

Assessment of the ideological and operational typologies developed by academics and practitioners demonstrates that the *Michigan Militia* and MOM represented the two faces of the militia movement as it developed during the 1990s. On the one hand, they have identified defensive and non-violent militias which leverage legitimate means in order to protect their members' civil liberties, and in general do not directly challenge the sovereignty of the federal government. On the other hand, they have identified offensive, violent, and underground militias which encourage their members to engage in direct attacks and actions against the federal government, including illegal initiatives and retaliatory attacks.[281]

The second type of militias, not surprisingly, were those which attracted most of the attention of local and national law enforcement because they used their military

---

[279] There were inspirational figures within the movement who gained significant influence, such as Linda Thompson, Samuel Sherwood, James (Bo) Gritz and others; most of them specialized in producing ideological and operational publications: see Neil, 76–90.
[280] Snow, 14.
[281] For discussion of this typology see Freilich, 14.

training in order to engage in illegal and violent activities. While an extensive analysis of the militias' violence is presented in the empirical section of this study, an initial overview makes clear that during the 1990s most of the violent militias were exposed while in their planning and operational preparation stage, such as: the Arizona-based *Viper Militia*, which was uncovered after its members had trained for two years and in the midst of advance planning to bomb the IRS, ATF, Police and National Guard Center facilities in Phoenix; the *Oklahoma Constitutional Militia*, whose members were arrested while preparing explosive devices to destroy the Southern Poverty Law Center (SPLC) offices and abortion clinics; the *Mountaineer Militia*, which plotted to blow up the FBI national fingerprint records center; and a cell which emerged from the *Third Continental Congress* (see above) and plotted an attack on various US Army facilities in Texas which they maintained incorporated UN facilities.[282] Successful plots were relatively rare and usually perpetrated by individuals or small cells associated with the fringe of the militia subculture, e.g., the OKBOMB; and the Atlanta Olympic Games attack perpetrated by Eric R. Rudolph.[283]

The public, media, and law enforcement associated the OKBOMB attack with the militia movement almost immediately, since McVeigh was linked to the *Michigan Militia* and similar groups in Arizona, and expressed the views advocated in militia propaganda. This association had a multilayer impact on the militia movement. The movement leaders were placed on the defensive; many of them were quick to claim that the attack was a government-sponsored ploy perpetrated in order to justify increasing scrutiny of the movement by authorities.[284] Others were critical of the media and government use of the event in order to de-legitimize the movement and to color it as racist, anti-Semitic and inherently violent.[285] On the other hand, the event greatly magnified the movement's public exposure, facilitating recruitment and expansion. Reports by SPLC and the ADL concluded that in late 1995 and early 1996 the movement consisted of more than 200 militias in more than 35 states.[286] Nonetheless, and despite the short-term

---

[282] See ADL, "Extremism in America: The Militia Movement,"
http://www.adl.org/learn/ext_us/militia_m.asp?xpicked=4&item=19 (accessed 3 November 2012).
[283] This issue will receive further discussion in chapter 5 of this study.
[284] For example, Linda Thompson asserted that "I definitely believe the government did the bombing. I mean who's got a track record of killing children?" ADL, *Beyond the Bombing: The Militia Menace Grows* (New York: ADL, 1995), 15.
[285] Neil Hamilton, 43–4.
[286] ADL (1995), *Beyond the Bombing*.

boost to its numbers, the overall trajectory of the movement was downward during the second half of the 1990s. The attack in Oklahoma led law enforcement organizations to increase their efforts to infiltrate and thwart militia group operations. Hundreds of militia members were arrested; many of them were prosecuted for the illegal manufacture and distribution of firearms, explosives and ammunition.[287] Dozens of violent plots were uncovered, and in general the authorities grew much less tolerant of paramilitary activities conducted by civilian associations. A growing number of states in the 1990s also enacted anti-paramilitary training statutes, which restrict unauthorized military-style training.[288]

Several other developments intensified the decline of the movement towards the 2000s. In the second half of the 1990s, the movement was swamped by millenarian conspiracy theories. Most of these theories included a variation of the following narrative: the collapse of the country's infrastructure during the first weeks of the year 2000 as a result of the Y2K software bug; the social and economic havoc which will follow will be exploited by the government to declare martial law and perpetrate mass violations of constitutional rights, ultimately resulting in the restoration of law and order with the assistance of international forces and their connivance in creating the NWO.[289] Many also argued that this scheme was supported by collaborators from among the major parties and from within the U.S. Armed Forces.

It is evident that the economic boom of the late 1990s, which was followed by the passage to 2000 without any catastrophe and the election of a conservative president, led to a dramatic decrease in the credibility of the movement and its leaders. The militia members who expected a watershed event that would substantiate their ideological foundations instead witnessed a rise in the standard of living and the election of a president identifying with small government, and strong and independent local authorities. For many militia members, America was on the right track; thus, the incentive to prepare for war against NWO forces evaporated. This is almost exactly the

---

[287] ADL, "Extremism in America: The Militia Movement".

[288] See e.g., Florida, Stat. ch. 870.06 (1994); Georgia, Code ann. § 38-2-277 (Harrison 1995); Iowa, Code § 29A.31 (1995); Kansas, Stat. Ann. § 48-203 (1994); Maine, Rev. Stat. Ann. tit. 37-B, § 342.2 (West 1996); Maryland, Ann. Code, Militia § 35 (1995); Nevada, Rev. Stat. § 203.080 (1995); North Carolina, Gen. Stat. § 127A-151 (1986 and Supp. 1996); West Virginia, Code § 15-1F-7 (1995); Wyoming, Stat. Ann. § 19-1-106 (Michie 1996).

[289] For further consideration of preparations of the Militias for the Millennium, see Norman Olson, "The Militia and Y2K"(1999) and Virginian Citizens Militia. *Y2K Policy Statement*, 6 March.

opposite of the developments which occurred in 2008—the election of a Democratic president with a liberal background; the economic recession; and the introduction of policies and reforms threatening the independence of local political authorities—which have led to what some claim is the revival of the militia movement. The scope and characteristics of this revival are analyzed in the empirical section of this study.

3.2.3 – The Christian Fundamentalist Movements: Organizational and Operational Development

Unlike the movements discussed previously, the fundamentalist movement's militant and violent nature was relatively late to develop. For many years the SMOs of the fundamentalist movement did not produce violent sub-groups, but rather functioned as a source of intellectual inspiration and a moral justification for the violent activities and operations of ideologically related movements. Hence, it is not surprising that many of the prominent ideologues of the white supremacist and anti-federalist movements intensively cooperated with—and at times saw themselves as part of—the fundamentalist movement. This dynamic allowed the penetration of non-identity ideas into the movement, and in many ways facilitated the narrowing of the gaps between the fundamentalist movement and other streams of the American far right. As with the anti-federalist movement, however, the fundamentalist movement was never able to develop an effective nation-wide organizational framework. This could be attributed to the inherent inability of highly charismatic and authoritarian pastors to share power with others, or to the tendency of each pastor to engage in the development of his creed, a dynamic which created difficulty in forming a consensual ideological paradigm. This corresponds with theoretical frameworks which emphasize the process whereby isolated constituencies—as is typical of the various Christian Identity churches—which have limited face-to-face interactions with other constituencies encourage non-federated SMOs.[290]

3.2.3.1 – The Operational and Organizational Development of the Christian Identity Movement

By the mid-nineteenth century the British-Israelite ideology had already crossed the Atlantic; the writings of John Wilson and Edward Hine had attracted the attention of a small but devoted group of adherents. Nonetheless, most of them—such as Pastor Joseph Wild from Brooklyn, or the Kansas-based novelist M. M Eshelman—were local

---

[290] McCarty and Zald.

figures who lacked the resources or the aspirations to found a nationwide theological movement.[291]

This dynamic began to change in late 1884 with the arrival of Hine to the Northeast and the Great Lakes areas on a five-year lecture tour he conducted among his American followers.[292] The tour, from which Hine produced published materials aimed specifically at his American audience, was a fillip for the emerging movement and spurred the further expansion of British-Israelite ideas in the United States.[293] Thus, in the late 1890s, British-Israelite congregations could be found in most of the major cities of the Northeast, as well as in the Midwest where the ideology attracted a significant number of evangelical Protestants. When Protestants moved in great numbers to the Far West in the late nineteenth and early twentieth centuries, California also became an important stronghold of the movement.

While absent a centralized organizational framework, several popular publications facilitated the crystallization of the movement's ideological principles, which in later years would become the ideological building blocks of the Identity movement. These publications, such as C. A. L Totten's *Our Race*, or A. A. Beauchamp's *Watchman of Israel*,[294] were also effective tools in the early 1920s for the expansion of the movement, and provided a platform for the rise of nationwide leaders. An instance of this is one of the more prolific contributors to the *Watchmen of Israel*, Reuben H. Sawyer, who became a prominent speaker for the movement throughout the West and Midwest, and one of the founders of the *British-Israelite World Federation*, the umbrella organization of the movement, which was established in London in 1920.[295] In the late 1920s Sawyer was joined by prolific writer and publisher Howard Rand, who was not only devoted to spreading British-Israelite ideas, but was also convinced of the need to form an organizational structure which would coordinate the activities of the movement's

---

[291] Barkun, 17–18.

[292] Alexander B. Grimaldy, *Memoirs, and a Selection of Letters from the Correspondence of Eduard Hine* (London: Robert Banks and Son, 1909), 20–50.

[293] Barkun, 18–19.

[294] Charles A. Totten, *Our Race: Its Origins and Destiny, A series of Studies on the Saxon Riddle* (New Haven: Our Race Publishing Company, 1891); Frank F. Gosset, *Race: The History of an Idea in America* (New York: Schocken, 1987), 191–2.

[295] Sawyer was also a KKK member during the early 1920s: this is of little surprise considering that these were the heydays of the second Klan. For his articles see e.g., Reuben H. Sawyer, "The American Idea," *Watchman of* Israel, 3 (April 1921), 114–15; Reuben H. Sawyer, "Who are the Americans?" *Watchman of* Israel, 3 (August 1921), 182–5.

different branches, as well as linking its ideological principles with modern-day political agendas.[296]

Rand's efforts bore fruit in 1930 when the first convention of the *Anglo-Saxon Federation of America* was held in Detroit, as well as in following years when branches of the federation were established in California, Illinois, Florida, Oregon, Washington, Idaho, Nevada, Utah, Michigan and in most states of the Northeast.[297] The rapid expansion was aided by the production of an immense amount of published material: close to fifty thousand pieces of relevant literature were produced in the early 1930s alone.[298] Use of print media and radio, during this period of extreme hopelessness and at the height of the Great Depression, increased the mobilization potential of millenarian and religious movements at that time. The rise of William J. Cameron to the presidency of the movement in the mid-1930s, with his excellent organizational and public relations skills and political and financial connections to Henry Ford and the Detroit business community, also provided the movement with significant momentum.[299]

Along with Rand, Cameron was responsible for the growing anti-Semitic tendencies in the movement and its sympathy and cooperation with the American right. He was highly active in producing anti-Semitic publications reliant on British-Israelite ideas, and formed a mechanism for the distribution of the Federation's material to prominent political operatives within the American political right.[300] There are various views, and contradicting evidence, regarding the way other members of the movement felt about these ideological and political shifts; it seems, however, that the growing dissatisfaction by some ultimately led to the replacement of Cameron in 1937 and the decision to relocate the federation's headquarters from Detroit—Cameron's power base—to Haverhill, Massachusetts. In any case, the federation as an effective organization deteriorated during WWII and the following decade. The departure of Cameron, the aging of its leadership, and the dramatic improvement of the economy in the 1950s made it difficult for the federation to recruit a new generation of followers.[301]

---

[296] Quarles, (2004), 54–5.

[297] Barkun, 30.

[298] Ibid.

[299] Barkun, 30–32.

[300] Probably the most popular platform for the dissemination of Anti-Semitic ideas was the *Independent*, which achieved infamy when it was sued for its *International Jew* series of publications: see Gerber, 20–22, 29–30.

[301] Barkun, 40–41.

Nonetheless, in terms of the massive amount of published material, organizational structure, and conceptual articulation between far-right and religious notions, the ideological and organizational foundation was secured for the emergence of Christian Identity.

The first Christian Identity groups emerged on the West Coast in the late 1940s. Their origins can be traced to a series of conventions that were organized between 1937 and 1947 in the northern Pacific by a British-Israelite association from Vancouver. These conferences led to the formation of a network of groups on the Pacific coast that was relatively isolated from the British Israelite World Federation, as well as its American branch. The isolation was not only a reflection of the geographical distance between the Pacific groups and the center of the federation in the East, but also of an ongoing political struggle and hostility between the Pacific branches of the movement and some of the East Coast associations, especially between the Vancouver and Toronto branches.[302] In any case, this isolation allowed the Pacific groups to depart from the traditional British-Israelite ideological tradition and to develop unique ideological notions focusing on extreme anti-Semitism, racial conspiracy theories and apocalyptic visions.

This new coalition of groups moved further from the British-Israelite ideological tradition with the rise of Gerald K. Smith to a leadership position within the movement. Smith was a Southern political operative who was the main aide to Louisiana Senator Huey P. Long during the Great Depression.[303] He moved to Los Angeles in the early 1950s and quickly became the major organizational force behind the emerging Identity movement via its own organization, *The Christian Nationalist Crusade*. Smith magnified the importance of anti-Semitic ideas in the movement's ideology and worked intensively to tighten its ties with the American political far-right by recruiting the movement for campaigns against the Civil Rights Movement and the perceived communist threat.[304] He was also able to mentor and nurture a new cadre of political and religious leaders such as Conrad Gaard, Jonathan Perkins, Bertrand Comparet and Wesley Swift.[305]

---

[302] Alma M. Hertherington, *70 Years Old!: An Outline History of Our Work Since 1909* (Burnaby, BC: Association of Covenant People, 1979), 1–10, 20.

[303] Quarles, (2004), 54–5.

[304] Barkun, 54–5.

[305] Glen Jeanstone, *Gerald K. Smith: Minister of Hate* (New Haven, Connecticut: Yale University, 1988), 99–100, 105–6.

Swift became the most influential ideologue of the Identity movement in its early days. He founded his church around 1948 under the name *Anglo-Saxon Christian Congregation*—which was quickly replaced by the name *The Church of Jesus Christ Christian*—in Lancaster, California. Very quickly it became clear that he was one of the more charismatic and talented speakers of the Identity movement as well as being a highly capable organizer who formed ties with other Identity associations.[306] These relations enabled him to engage in frequent lectures tours all over the West Coast and the Midwest, as well as to broaden the exposure of his ideas dramatically. This was also facilitated by Swift's popular weekly radio show and distribution of audio tapes of his lectures.[307] In his lectures he did not rely only on biblical texts to justify the racial superiority of the Aryan people; he also elevated the anti-Semitic rhetoric of the movement to new heights, as typified by a statement he made in the early 1950s in one of his lectures: "All Jews must be destroyed. I prophesy that before November 1953 there will not be a Jew in the United States, and by that I mean a Jew that will be able to walk or talk."[308]

Swift's blunt anti-Semitism also made him a popular figure among members of the KKK and other white supremacy groups, many of whom had found their way into the different organizations Swift helped to establish and to sponsor in the 1950s and the 1960s. These organizations incorporated radical ideological ideas and also were involved in radical political activism and violence. The *Christian Defense League* (CDL), for example, was involved in paramilitary activities, with unsubstantiated accusations of the involvement of CDL members in violent attacks against minorities, and a plan to assassinated Rev. Martin Luther King.[309] While the CDL declined in the late 1960s, two of its main leaders, Colonel William Potter Gale, and Richard Butler, would become the face of the movement from the late 1960s to the late 1980s via their respective organizations: Gale's *Posse Comitatus* and its militant offshoots, and Butler's *Church of Jesus Christ Christian* and its political wing, the *Aryan Nations*.

From an ideological and operational perspective, the *Posse Comitatus* shared some similarities with the 1990s *militias* and set the stage for the more contemporary *Sovereign*

---

[306] Barkun, 54–5.
[307] Jeanstone, 99–100, 24–5.
[308] Levitas, 25.
[309] Kaplan, 49.

Citizens Movement. Its origins could be traced to Colonel William Potter Gale's *Ministry of Christ Church* and its journal "Identity."[310] During 1967 Gale used the journal's pages to endorse an emerging tax rebellion movement and its leader, a Kansas based building constructor by the name of Arthur Julius Porth.[311] After the latter was arrested in 1970, Gale organized rallies, seminars and a public campaign for his release. This campaign triggered a momentum in terms of public support, which, along with the vacuum created by the death of Swift and the arrest of the *Minuteman's* leader Robert Depugh that year, seems to have driven Gale to establish a new organization which would continue the struggle against what he saw as the attempt by governmental authorities to impose inappropriate practices, values and norms on the American people, or in his own words, to (prevent the Congress from) subverting the Constitution of the United States and violating the Laws of its Christian Constitutional Republic.[312]

What emerged was a network of *Posse* associations which combined racist and anti-Semitic Identity ideas and practices with active hostility and militancy towards the federal authorities and especially the IRS. Between the years 1972-1974, the organization spread significantly and chapters were formed in Oregon, Idaho, Michigan, Alaska, Washington (state), Virginia and Arkansas. Many of them however were relatively small and founded by individuals who believed this would help them fight their own personal struggle with the authorities.[313] While some members in these chapters did not just engage in publicizing their beliefs and ideas, but were also willing to practice them and "protect" their rights with deeds, a fact which triggered several violent incidents involving representatives of the federal authorities and workers unions, overall it is difficult to claim that *Posse* activities escalated into an organized violent campaign. Hence, while the organization gained considerable attention from the authorities and media exposure until its decline in the late 1970s and early 1980s, it was never more than a loose network of frustrated entrepreneurs and farmers who found a common "enemy" and usually engaged in active protest. The picture was fundamentally different however in the case of the *Aryan Nations* and its offshoots.

When Swift died in 1970, Richard Butler established his own *Church of Jesus Christ Christian* in a deserted compound near Hayden Lake, Idaho after his attempt to be

---

[310] Levitas, 97–8.
[311] See, e.g., William Potter Gale, "Enemy Within," *Identity*, 5(1) (1969), 6.
[312] Levitas, 108–10.
[313] Levitas, 139–53.

recognized as Swift's successor was rejected. His goal was to "[e]xpand the Kingdom Identity program and form the foundation for a call to the nation or Aryan Nations."[314] Shortly after the move to Idaho, Butler and his close associate Robert Miles, who headed the *Mountain Church of Jesus*, agreed to form an organization that would promote the idea of transforming the "white bastion"—most of the states of Washington, Oregon, Montana and Wyoming—into the base of a future Aryan polity. This organization became known as the *Aryan Nations Church of Jesus Christ Christian*, shortened to *Aryan Nations* (AN).[315]

Under Butler's charismatic leadership in the 1970s and early 1980s, the AN quickly expanded its wings by establishing chapters in other states and promoting various mobilization initiatives. Maybe the best known initiative was the "World Congresses of Aryan Nations," which were basically summer festivals focusing on white supremacy themes, and which also included paramilitary and weapons training and attracted several hundred members.[316] The annual youth conventions were another initiative that was eventually followed by the formation of the "Aryan Nations Academy" which included several dozen full-time students from pre-school to eighth grade.[317] Relying on the growing number of AN members serving long prison sentences during the 1980s, the AN was also highly active in recruiting support from the inmate populations in correctional facilities.[318]

While all of the above strategies expedited the spread of Identity ideas and elevated public awareness of the organization, the most important element that transformed the AN and its Idaho compound into the organizational, ideological and operational center of the Identity and the broader American far right—or as Butler termed it: "The International Headquarters of the White Race"—was the fact that the Idaho compound became a safe haven for many of the leaders of the various far right associations in the

---

[314] Quarles, (2004), 133.

[315] See ADL, "Extremism in America: Aryan Nations/Church of Jesus Christ Christian," *Anti-Defamation League,* http://www.adl.org/learn/ext_us/aryan_nations.asp?xpicked=3&item=an (accessed 3 November 2012).

[316] Evelyn Schlatter, *Aryan Cowboys: White Supremacists and the Search for a New Frontier, 1970–2000* (Austin, Texas: University of Texas Press, 2006), 66.

[317] G. Gordon Liddy, CDR James G. Liddy, J. Michael Barrett, Joel Selanikio, *Fight Back: Tackling Terrorism, Liddy Style* (New York: St. Martin's Griffin, 2006), 75.

[318] Schlatter, 67.

country.[319] It was a place which was isolated and distant enough to discourage the intrusion of law enforcement, media and the general public, and which also offered the freedom and intellectual stimulation of a wilderness environment. Thus, major ideologues of the American far right, figures such as KKK's Louis Beam, WAR's Tom Metzger, and even the founder of the *Montana Militia*, Jon Trochmann, felt free to develop their ideological visions, to improve coordination and cooperation, and to mobilize new recruits while spending significant time at the AN compound in Idaho.[320]

Ideologically the AN promoted what could be termed radical localism. In many ways similar to the visions promoted by the militias in the 1990s, these ideas centered around the desire to create a network of Aryan farm communities that would be run according to "Biblical/Aryan" laws independent of federal authorities.[321] However, unlike the case of the militias, the idea behind this vision was driven less by hostility towards the authorities, and more by the desire to promote racial segregation. The latter was a reflection of the AN's militant and activist version of Identity's traditional anti-Semitic and racial principles which, while still based on a revisionist interpretation of biblical texts, was also facilitated by the incorporation of national socialist elements and symbols.[322] The following statement by Pastor August Kreis, the current formal leader of AN, explains this situation: "We, as your elect, will carry out your wrath against your enemies on this, the great battlefield, called earth…We look forward to the destruction of your enemies on this earth and to the establishment of your kingdom."[323] In another statement, he was more explicit: "We firmly believe that until every last Jew Yehudi-Shataan is dead, there will be no peace in earth. There is no room for negotiation; we want no peace with them; there is no living with them. We will accept nothing less for Edo/Esau Jewry than explained in Matthew 13."[324]

Some AN members who were exposed to these statements and texts engaged in violent and illegal activities. Some acted alone and without organizational assistance, such as Buford Furrow. A former AN security guard, Furrow fired more than 70 rounds from a submachine gun at children and teenagers at the North Valley Jewish Community

---

[319] Quarles, (2004), 133–4.
[320] George Michael, *Confronting Right-Wing Extremism and Terrorism in the USA* (New York: Routledge, 2003), 46; Kaplan, 18.
[321] Barkun, 231–2.
[322] Barkun, 233–4.
[323] Quarles, (2004), 134.
[324] Ibid.

Center in Los Angeles, California on August 10, 1998; he injured three boys and a teenage girl.[325] Others exercised violence with organizational support. A famous example of such an organization was *The Order*, the revolutionary group which Earl Turner joined, as described in the *Turner Diaries*.[326] It was founded in 1983 by Robert Mathews, an Identity activist from Idaho with the aim of forming a small cell in Arizona which would first require financial resources, and would then engage in guerrilla warfare against the federal government. Specifically, it would target what it called the ZOG: the Zionist Occupation Government, which in turn would ignite a mass uprising. After recruiting several dozen members, mostly from the AN but also from other far-right groups including the NA and the KKK, *The Order* initiated a campaign of counterfeiting, armed robberies and violent attacks carried out between 1983 and 1986.[327] The most successful robbery was of a Brinks armored vehicle near Ukiah, California which netted $3.8 million. Other violent attacks conducted by *The Order* were: the assassination of Alan Berg, a Jewish liberal radio host at KOA radio, as a response to Berg's tendency to ridicule the far right; the bombing of a pornographic theater in Seattle, Washington, and of a synagogue in Boise, Idaho in April 1984; and the bombing of the house of a Catholic priest in August 1986 in Coeur D'alene, Idaho.[328]

While some members of *The Order* had criminal backgrounds, they had limited operational experience regarding the different challenges concerned with operating a clandestine group. It is therefore not surprising that the FBI succeeded in penetrating the group and detaining most of its members in less than a year after it was formed. Mathews was located in December 1984 at Whidbey Island in Washington State, and was killed during a shootout with FBI agents. No less than 75 people, including 48 who

---

[325] CNN Justice, "Furrow pleads guilty to shootings, will avoid death penalty, get life without parole," 24 January (2001), http://articles.cnn.com/2001-01-24/justice/furrow.plea.crim_1_furrow-shooting-rampage-ileto?_s=PM:LAW (accessed 3 November 2012).

[326] *The Turner Diaries*, a text initially published in a serial form by the NA's *Attack* magazine, and in 1978 as a book, was authored by William Pierce, the founder of the *National Alliance*. It tells the story of Earl Turner, an American who joins a revolutionary group fighting against the flood of racial integration and gun control legislation. The book, one of the most popular texts within the far right scene in the US, describes the group's violent attacks against symbols of the federal government and concludes with Turner crashing an airplane armed with a nuclear warhead into the Pentagon. See - Andrew Macdonald, Turner Diaries (New York: Barricade, 2003). The novel is also available online: SolarGeneral.com, White Nationalist News Portal, Turner Diaries.

[327] Dobratz and Shanks-Meile, 192.

[328] Ibid.

were active members of the group, were convicted on numerous charges related to *The Order* activities.[329]

Another well-known and violent group which arose from the Identity movement at that time and had close relations with AN and *New Order* was the *Covenant, The Sword and the Arm of the Lord* (CSA). In the early 1980s members of the group were mainly involved in a series of insurance fraud, arson attacks and robberies in order to garner resources for what it saw as the inevitable "Armageddon."[330] In late 1983 the group escalated its attacks with a series of bombings of civilian infrastructure, including water supplies and electric facilities. In mid-1985 the FBI and other agencies took control of the group's compound, located close to Bull Shoal Lake in Arkansas. Following the trials of the group's members it was revealed that they were planning a mass-scale poisoning operation of the country's main water supplies.[331]

Since the early 1990s, the AN's prominent position within the Identity movement eroded. While Butler's age and declining health played a role in this, the main cause was Butler's success in nurturing a skilled cadre of potential future leaders and operatives. Many of them preferred to leave the AN and to establish their own churches and organizations. For instance, Butler's Chief of Staff, Carl Franklin, and AN's security chief Wayne Jones established the *Church of Jesus Christ Christian of Montana*; and Charles and Betty Tate—chiefs of AN's printing operations—left to promote a new group in North Carolina.[332] Furthermore, several successful civilian law suits against AN members in the late 1990s and early 2000s—including a verdict which forced the organization to pay a sum of $6.3 million to Victoria and Jason Keenan, a mother and son who were attacked by AN members—crippled the organization financially.[333]

---

[329] Kevin Flynn and Gary Gerhardt, *The Silent Brotherhood: Inside America's Racist* Underground (New York: Free Press, 1995), 442–6.

[330] Jessica Stern, "The Covenant, the Sword, and the Arm of the Lord," in Jonathan Tucker ed. *Toxic Terror* (Cambridge: MIT Press, 2000), 139–57; Quarles, (2004), 135–8.

[331] Ibid.

[332] See ADL, "Extremisim in America: Richard Butler," *Anti-Defamation League,* http://www.adl.org/learn/ext_us/butler.asp?xpicked=2&item=butler (accessed 3 November 2012).

[333] For the verdict summary see Southern Poverty Law Center, "Case Docket: Keenan v. Aryan Nations," Southern Poverty Law Center 9 July (2000), http://www.splcenter.org/get-informed/case-docket/keenan-v-aryan-nations (accessed 3 November 2012).

The emergence of competing organizations also facilitated organizational and ideological fragmentation within the Identity movement and challenged the status of AN and Butler (Butler died in 2004, leaving the organization under the leadership of August Kries III, with smaller factions still operating in Texas and New York). The most prominent of these competing organizations was established by Pastor Pete Peters, who via his Colorado based *La Porta Church of Christ,* and its outreach arm *Scriptures for America* became one of the most notable speakers and leaders of the Identity movement.[334]

Although *La Porta Church of Christ* had been founded earlier in 1977, only in the late 1980s and early 1990s did Peters begin to expand his influence within the Identity movement. He became highly effective in promoting the Identity arsenal of extreme anti-Semitic, apocalyptic conceptions and white supremacy ideology via the mass media, including the *Scriptures for America* short-wave radio program and website, dissemination of audiocassette tapes of his sermons and those of other Identity preachers.[335] Nonetheless, he was usually perceived as more moderate and less militant than his AN counterparts. By hosting Scriptures for America Bible retreats, family Bible Camp conferences, seminars and other activities, Peters, like Butler before him, was able to transform his Colorado compound into an organizational and ideological hub for the movement, attracting prominent Identity and other far-right figures.

A reflection of Peters's rising status was illustrated in his ability to gather more than 160 far right leaders in Estes Park, Colorado following the Ruby Ridge crisis. Here he escalated his criticism of the federal authorities and was able to position himself as one of the prominent leaders of the American far right and the Identity movement. For many years the authorities in Colorado sought means to narrow Peters's influence, including charging him with violation of election law after he purchased $1,040 worth of radio and newspaper ads to help to defeat a ballot initiative extending civil rights protection to gays and lesbians in Fort Collins, Colorado. Such measures served to elevate his status within the movement as a martyr persecuted by the government.[336]

---

[334] Dobratz and Shanks-Meile, 80; ADL, "Extremism in America: Peter J. "Pete" Peters," *Anti-Defamation League,* http://www.adl.org/learn/ext_us/peters.asp?learn_cat=extremism&learn_subcat=extremism_in_america&xpicked=2&item=8 (accessed 3 November 2012).
[335] See examples at *Dragon Slayer* Newsletter 2005, vol.2; *Dragon Slayer* Newsletter 2005, vol.3.
[336] See ADL report on Peters: ADL, "Extremism in America: Peter J. "Pete" Peters".

While further examination of the current status of the movement is provided in the empirical section of this study, it should be noted that the movement continued to maintain its relatively fragmented nature, with more than 60 ministries and around 50 thousand supporters.

3.2.3.2 – Army of God and Anti-Abortion Violence

A review of the history of domestic political violence in the United States identifies 1977 as the year in which anti-abortion violence made itself apparent, with several arson attacks against abortion clinics in St. Paul; Burlington, Vermont; and Omaha.[337] The level of violence intensified dramatically in the early 1980s when Army of God members adopted extreme tactics which included kidnappings of abortion clinic owners and employees, incendiary and pipe bombing of abortion clinics, and the assassination of prominent medical personnel in Florida, Washington DC, Virginia, Maryland, and other states on the East Coast. Overall, during the years 1977–2000, anti-abortionists perpetrated more than 80 successful arson attacks, 31 attacks with various explosive devices, almost 30 incidents of chemical vandalism, and approximately 10 assassination attempts.[338]

In most cases the violence was initiated by individuals or small cells of 2–3 people, indicating that pro-life violence was a product of a violent subculture comprised of isolated cells of anti-abortionists and, in many cases, individual perpetrators.[339] Until recently there has been no evidence of the existence of nation-wide organizational infrastructure other than the *Army of God*. While there are still different accounts regarding the organizational structure of AOG, it is likely that the group was constituted by a loose association of anti-abortion activists which formed in the early 1980s.[340] The name was probably used for the first time by Don Benny in 1982 when he and two partners kidnapped an Illinois abortion provider and his wife. After the couple was released and Benny and his associates were arrested, it was determined that they had also been involved in several cases of arson attacks against abortion clinics.[341] Other famous members of the group were Michael Bray, Kenneth Shields and Thomas Spinks:

---

[337] Baird-Windle and Bader, 47–53.
[338] Hewitt.
[339] Jennifer L. Jefferis, *Armed for Life* (Santa Barbara, California: Praeger, 2011), 23–35.
[340] For a comprehensive analysis of AOG structure, see Jefferis.
[341] Baird-Windle and Bader, 47–53.

the three were responsible for the firebombing of at least ten abortion clinics in DC, Maryland and Virginia. After his arrest, Bray continued publicly to support violent attacks against the abortion industry. Erich Robert Rudolph—known for hiding a bomb at the Centennial Olympic Park during the 1996 Atlanta Olympic Games—was involved in several bombings of abortion clinics; and Shelly Shannon was arrested in 1993 for attempted murder of an abortion physician.[342]

In the mid to late 1980s, the group distributed a text to its members which would enhance its visibility dramatically among anti-abortionists and would become their ideological and operational bible. Besides clarifying the ideological tenets of a violent anti-abortionist avant-garde, the *AOG Manual* also includes detailed operational instructions for how to conduct attacks against the abortion industry and its supporters, including: methods for disrupting the operation of clinics, such as gluing locks and damaging clinical equipment with butyric acid; how to prepare different types of explosive devices, including plastic explosives, and deploy them to maximize damage; and operational knowledge useful for the murder of individuals involved in the abortion industry.[343] To summarize, the manual justified and provided comprehensive instructions for the use of extreme violence in order to "disarm the murder weapons."[344] What has happened to the violent anti-abortionist stream in the last decade? Is it still a threat? How can we explain its rise during the 1980s and 1990s? These questions are discussed in the following part of the study, which focuses on an empirical analysis of the violent American far right.

---

[342] Mark Juergensmeyer, *Terror in the Mind of God: The Global Rise of Religious Violence* (Berkeley, California: University of California Press, 2000), 30–31.
[343] Jefferis, 54–5.
[344] Ibid.

Part 2 – Empirical and Theoretical Foundations: Explaining American Far-Right Violence

4. Empirical Picture: General Overview of the American Violent Far Right

4.1 – Methodological Aspects and Data Gathering

To decipher the current landscape of the violent American far-right, a dataset was constructed specifically for this study. The dataset documents all violent attacks that: (1) were perpetrated by groups or individuals affiliated with far-right associations; and/or (2) were intended to promote ideas compatible with far-right ideology, based on the ideological analysis presented in the first part of this study. Many scholars treat these acts as terrorism.[345] However, in the current study the more generalized designation of political violence is used to describe far-right violent activities, as this term is broader than terrorism. While there is no consensual definition of terrorism among academics or practitioners, most agree that it consists of violent acts perpetrated to promote specific collective national, religious, or communal ideas in a political context and in civilian settings.[346] Most scholars also emphasize the psychological and symbolic nature of terrorism and its ability to exploit violence in order to shape political discourse. Many of the attacks in the dataset are compatible with all of these criteria. However, some of them, while exhibiting a clear political context, lack the instrumental use of violence. In other words, while the political motivation of the act is detectable, how it is supposed to impact the broader political discourse is much less clear; for this reason the symbolic element identifiable in the majority of terrorist campaigns is absent from a significant number of far-right violent attacks.

The dataset includes violence against human targets as well as property, and contains details regarding: (1) the date of the attack; (2) perpetrator(s) characteristics and their organizational and ideological affiliation; (3) target characteristics; (4) implications of the attack (number of fatalities and injured, and whether it was completed successfully); (5) geographical aspects; (6) tactical details; and (7) a concise description of the attack. Data gathering was based on a variety of resources including relevant information

---

[345] For example, Blee presents a conceptualization of "racial terrorism." See Kathleen M. Blee, "Women and Organized Racial Terrorism in the United States," *Studies in Conflict & Terrorism*, 28:5 (2005), 421–33.
[346] A useful review of the relevant literature can be found in Bruce Hoffman, *Inside Terrorism*, (Revised and Expanded Edition), (New York: Columbia University Press, 2006), 1–41; Leonard Weinberg, Ami Pedahzur, and Sivan Hirsch, "The Challenges of Conceptualizing Terrorism," *Terrorism and Political Violence* 17(1) (2004), 1–17; Peter A. Schmid, and Albert Jongman, *Political Terrorism* (Amsterdam: North Holland Publishing, 1988), 1–38.

drawn from the Global Terrorism Dataset;[347] the SPLC hate crime dataset;[348] informative reports by various relevant organizations such as SPLC, ADL, RSCAR;[349] relevant academic texts; and various media source datasets, e.g., Lexis-Nexis. The consolidated dataset includes information on 4420 violent incidents that occurred between 1990 and 2012 within US borders, and which caused 670 fatalities and injured 3053 people.[350]

While our dataset is probably one of the most comprehensive accumulations of data on far-right violence in the United States, several limitations of the data should be noted. First, the quality of, and accessibility to, data on hate crimes and far right violence has improved during the last two decades: we need to take this into consideration when interpreting findings relating to fluctuations in levels of violence. Second, we need to take into account the differences between states pertaining to cultural norms and legal practices which impact upon the level of visibility of crimes: this can be understood as a ratio of criminal acts to reported crimes, which is often extremely difficult or impossible to determine. Such factors can distort findings relating to the geographical dispersion of violence. Finally, discrepancies exist between the dataset used by this study and other existing hate crimes datasets. This may be a result of differential or failed categorization, whereby violent incidents involving parties with different racial/ethnic affiliation but lacking clear evidence of far-right ideological motivation or association were not included.

The following section comprises an overview of the violence produced by the American far-right, pointing out major trends and initial conclusions. Following this is an assessment of the implications of the findings from a theoretical and analytical perspective.

---

[347] The GTD is being managed by the National Consortium for the Study of Terrorism and Responses to Terrorism (START) at the University of Maryland. For more information, see *Global Terrorism Databse,* http://www.start.umd.edu/gtd/ (accessed 3 November 2012).

[348] For more information about the Southern Poverty Law Center's Hate Crime dataset, see *Hate Incidents,* http://www.splcenter.org/get-informed/hate-incidents (accessed 3 November 2012).

[349] The Stephen Roth Institute for the Study of Contemporary Anti-Semitism and Racism explains that it "is a resource for information, provides a forum for academic discussion, and fosters continuing research on issues related to Anti-Semitic and racist theories and manifestations": "About the Institute: Mission Statement," http://www.tau.ac.il/Anti-Semitism/default.htm (accessed 3 November 2012).

[350] The decision to choose 1990 as the starting point for the dataset is because the existing literature provides relatively good coverage of the trends within the American violent far right up until the early 1990s; however, since then, the coverage is much more limited.

4.2.1 – The Development of American Far-Right Violence: Political Context

Figure 1 presents the number of attacks initiated by far-right groups/individuals per year since 1990.

Figure 1 - Attacks Initiated by Far-Right Groups/Individuals per Year

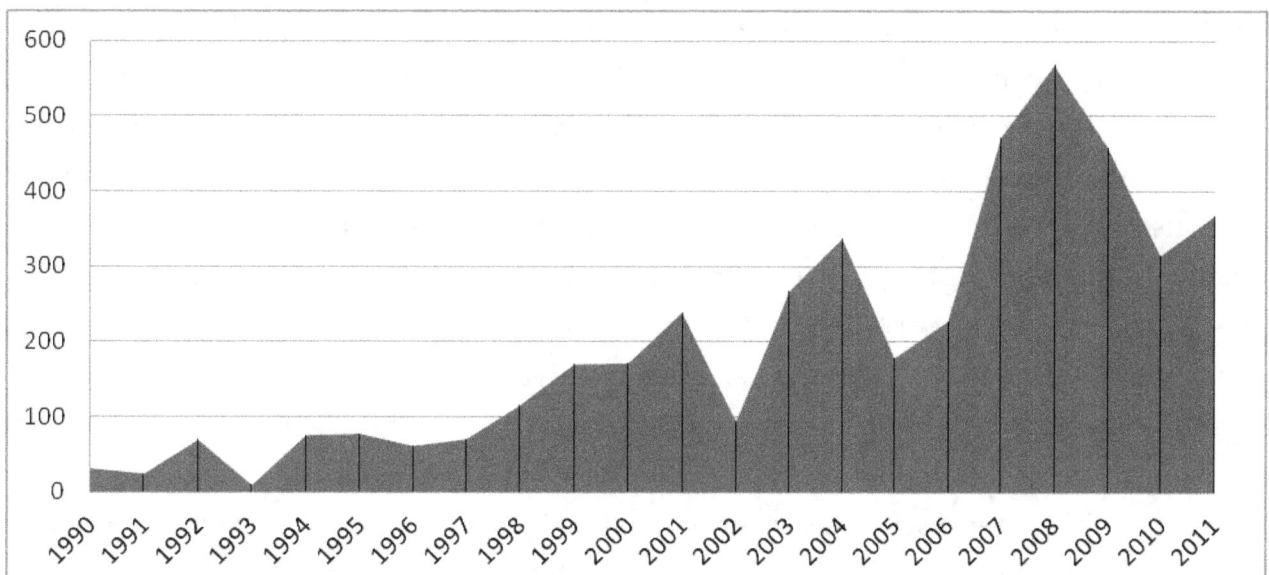

As can be seen, while there are variations over the years, the overall trend is very clear: from the early 1990s until 2008 there has been a clear increase in the number of attacks. Fourteen of the 21 years covered in this analysis witnessed more attacks than the previous year. Although in the 1990s the average number of attacks per year was 70.1, the average number of attacks per year in the first 11 years of the twenty-first century was 307.5, a rise of more than 400%.

Other initial insights can be extracted from the data. To begin with, presidential election years and the preceding year are characterized by an increase of far-right violence. For example, the years 1999 and 2000 saw an increase of almost 70% of the number of attacks recorded in 1998. The years 2003 and 2004 witnessed an increase of over 300% of the number of attacks in 2002. And the years 2007 and 2008 saw an increase of more than 100% of those for 2006. In regard to the 1992 elections, the increase occurred only in the election year. The trend appears to repeat itself in 2011, although it would be wise to wait until the end of 2012 before confirming this. A decline in the number of attacks can be detected only after elections. In 1993 there was a more than 700% decline from the 1992 figures; in 2005, a more than an 80% decline from 2004 occurred, and in 2009 there was a decrease of almost 30% from 2008 numbers. After the 2000 elections, the decline was visible only in 2002.[351]

These findings suggest that, in general, far-right groups and individuals are more inclined to engage in violence in a contentious political climate. This helps to explain the lack of increase in the level of violence during 1996, the least-competitive elections of the last 22 years. Several possible explanations may be offered: (1) Far-right groups assume that during election years the public is more receptive to political messages, including those conveyed via violent activism; (2) The competitive nature of the political environment during election years encourages engagement in political activism (see also Chenoweth, 2010) and provides more resources and opportunities; (3) The inability of far-right groups to penetrate the political system via legitimate means, as well as the marginality of their ideas, is even more sharply emphasized during electoral years. This further encourages the use of alternative means to promote their ideological agenda. The relatively informal, opportunity based and unorganized nature of far-right violence in the last two decades may make the third explanation more credible. In any case, the findings represent a contrasting perspective to prevalent perceptions regarding the association between political violence and democratic practices. Within the policy and academic realms there is a tendency to assume that democratic processes are an effective mechanism to discourage groups from engaging in violent political activism, since the democratic process provides non-violent alternatives for advancing political agendas.[352] However, the case of the American far-right indicates that under particular conditions the democratic process encourages violence.[353]

Looking at the impact of other political indicators helps in further deciphering the political context of far-right violence. Figure 2 illustrates the congruence between the composition of the legislative branch and the level of violence produced by the far right. The figure and analysis in this context also include data on attacks before the 1990s,

---

[351] Christopher Hewitt's chronology, which also documents far-right terrorism prior to the time captured by the dataset of this study, appears to demonstrate that the trend of increased violence during election years holds for most of the 1980s, as both 1980 and 1984 saw an approximate 100% rise in the number of attacks. In 1988 such a trend is not visible: see Hewitt.

[352] See e.g., Leonard Weinberg, "Terrorism and Democracy: Illness and Cure?" *Global Dialogue*, 8(3-4) (2006), http://www.worlddialogue.org/content.php?id=383 (accessed 3 November 2012).

[353] This conclusion accords with a number of relevant studies published recently: see Erica Chenoweth, "Democratic Competition and Terrorist Activity," *The Journal of Politics*, 72(1) (2010), 16–30.

based on Hewitt's chronology.[354] At first glimpse it appears as if the partisan composition of the Senate and the House has limited effect on trends in violence. For example, under a Democratic-controlled House in the first half of the 1960s and in the second half of the 2000s, we can see relatively high levels violence; while many years under Democratic-control also saw a dramatic decline in violence: see, e.g., the 1970s and 2009–2010.

Figure 2 – Far-Right Violence and the Composition of the Legislative Branch

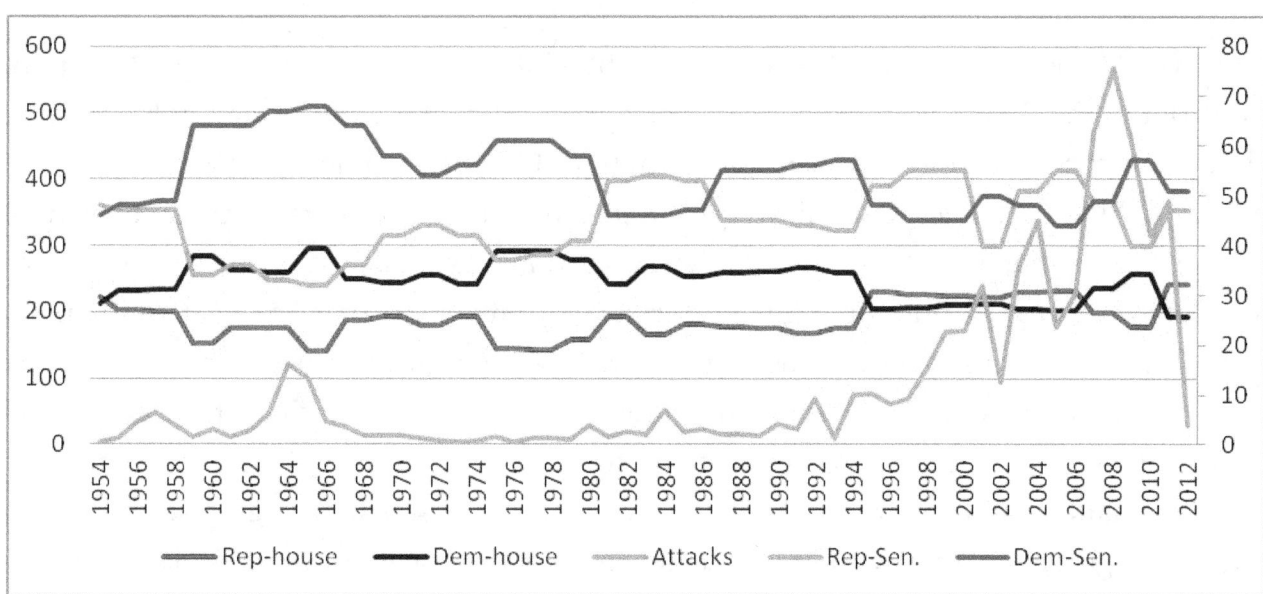

Nevertheless, statistical analysis of correlations, rather than only levels of violence under each administration, provides significant results which are not immediately apparent. The number of Democratic senators ($\alpha=-.271^*$)[355] and congressmen/women ($\alpha=-.411^{**}$) is negatively correlated with the number of attacks per year, whereas positive correlation of the latter exists with the number of Republican senators ($\alpha=.222^*$) and representatives ($\alpha=.413^{**}$).[356] An additional multivariate (stepwise) regression analysis reveals that the single most significant factor is the number of Republicans in the House ($\beta=.41^{**}$, $R^2=.17^{**}$).

---

[354] See Hewitt.

[355] In this and in the presentations of findings the level of statistical significance is represented as follow - *p<.05, **p<.01, ***p<.001.

[356] The level of significance here was .096, but since the gaps in the Senate between the two parties are traditionally relatively small, it still appears to indicate a significant correlation.

The correlation between increased conservative political power and far right violent activism need not imply causality. It is possible that far-right groups may feel that conservative political authorities are more tolerant of their activities, or believe that their actions have the potential to embolden their representatives to pursue an extreme right agenda. It is equally possible that increased levels of violence might be caused by relative deprivation, which occurs when the high expectations of far-right activists during a conservative legislature are not fulfilled. The deprivation explanation is less likely to occur under Democratic-controlled legislature since the expectations are low.

The correlation between the level of far-right violence and the identity of the party controlling the executive branch is weaker than the linkage between far-right violence and the composition of the legislature, although it is in the same direction. During the period 1990–2011, two Republican presidents and two Democratic presidents held office; the former for 10 years and the latter for 12 years. The average number of incidents per year during the terms of Republican presidents was 243.6, in comparison to 163 during the terms of Democrat presidents. Although they are much smaller, the gaps in the sample remain when using Hewitt's chronology to include the years 1954–1989. However, these are not statistically significant in any of the cases. While the limited quantity of data may contribute to the absence of statistical significance, overall the findings are in line with the conclusion that the level of violence is positively correlated with a conservative political environment.

So far the political context of far right violence has been examined in relation to the characteristics of formal political institutions. However, can we also attribute the increase in the level of violence during particular timeframes to specific policy initiatives or other developments in the political arena? This question is relevant for two reasons. First, some studies on radicalization of counterculture communities, i.e., their tendency to slide to violent activism, found significant correlation between the occurrence of political events or the initiation of governmental policies which had the potential to pose a threat to the counterculture way of life, and the tendency of community members to engage in violent activism.[357] Second, many of the texts that analyzed the history of the American far right tended to refer to such linkages. For

---

[357] Jerrold M. Post, "Terrorist Psycho-logic: Terrorist Behaviour as a Product of Psychological Forces," in Walter Reich ed. *The Origins of Terrorism* (Washington: Woodrow Wilson Center Press, 1990), 33; Juergensmeyer; Walter Laqueur, *The New Terrorism* (Oxford: Oxford University Press, 1999), 81–2.

example, the US Supreme Court rulings in 1954 against "separate but equal" policies in the education system, and in 1955, ordering district-level racial integration in the school system, are usually used to explain the recovery of the KKK in the mid-1950s.[358]

The main problem with many of these contentions is that they lack a comparative, systematic perspective and devolve to a tautological argument, drawing a bull's eye around the arrow, so-to-speak. To avoid anecdotal evidence and provide a methodical assessment of possible correlations, the linkages between civil rights on the one hand with abortion legislation and Supreme Court decisions on the other, will be assessed in a systematic way.

Table 1 includes a list of all relevant federal legislation, Supreme Court decisions and executive orders related to minority civil rights, abortion policies and federal gun control legislation. In each case the table attempts to provide information on the visible impact on the level of far right violence. Cases in which an effect was visible are marked in gray.

Table 1 - Far-Right Violence and Civil-right legislation/SC decisions/Executive Orders

Year	Details	Far-right violence
1954-55	***Brown v. Board of Education***: Chief Justice Earl Warren, reading his first major opinion from the bench, said: "We conclude, unanimously, that in the field of public education the doctrine of 'separate but equal' has no place. Separate educational facilities are inherently unequal." ***Brown v. Board II***: the Supreme Court held that school systems must abolish their racially dual systems, and should do so "with all deliberate speed."	Significant rise in far-right violence in the following years (1956–57), when the decisions were formally implemented. Reemergence of the KKK.
1956	The Supreme Court, without comment, affirmed a lower court ruling declaring segregation of the Montgomery bus system illegal, giving a major victory to Rosa Parks, Martin Luther King, Jr., and the thousands of anonymous African Americans who had sustained the bus boycott in the face of violence and intimidation.	Significant rise in far-right violence in the following years (1956-57), when the decisions were formally implemented. Reemergence of the KKK.
1963	**Equal Pay Act** - prohibits sex-based pay differentials in jobs.	No effect expected, no effect found.

---

[358] Quarles, (1999), 40.

1964	**Civil Rights Act** - Title VII prohibits employment discrimination based on race, sex, national origin, or religion. Title VI prohibits public access discrimination, leading to school desegregation. Title VIII is the original "federal fair housing law," amended in 1988.	Significant rise in the level of violence.
1965	**Executive Order 11246** - Affirmative action requirements of government contractors and subcontractors.	Significant rise in the level of violence.
1967	**ADEA** prohibits age discrimination for 40–65 year olds, amended in 1986 to remove the 65 year-old age cap.	No effect expected, no effect found.
1968	**Architectural Barriers Act** - requires accessibility for disabled in buildings and facilities financed with federal funds.	No effect expected, no effect found.
1968	**Gun Control Legislation in 1968** - prohibits transfers to minors and mail order sales, requires that guns carry serial numbers; implemented a tracking system to determine the purchaser of a gun whose make, model, and serial number are known. It also prohibited gun ownership by convicted felons.	No effect found.
1968	In *Jones v. Alfred H. Mayer Co.*, the Supreme Court held that the Civil Rights Act of 1866 bans racial discrimination in housing by private, as well as governmental, housing providers.	No effect found.
1971	In *Griggs v. Duke Power Co.*, the Supreme Court ruled that Title VII of the 1964 Civil Rights Act prohibits not only intentional job discrimination, but also employer practices that have a discriminatory effect on minorities and women. The Court held that tests and other employment practices that disproportionately screened out African American job applicants at the Duke Power Company were prohibited when the tests were not shown to be job-related.	No effect found.
1973	In *Roe v. Wade*, the Court ruled that a right to privacy under the due process clause of the 14th Amendment extended to a woman's decision to have an abortion, but that the right must be balanced against the state's two legitimate interests in regulating abortions: protecting prenatal life and protecting women's health. Arguing that these state interests became stronger over the course of a pregnancy, the Court resolved this balancing test by tying state regulation of abortion to the trimester of pregnancy, so that a person has a right to abortion until viability. The Roe decision defined "viable" as being "potentially able to live outside the mother's womb, albeit with artificial aid", adding that viability "is usually placed at about seven months (28 weeks) but may occur earlier, even at 24 weeks".	No effect found.
1973	**§504 of the Rehab Act** - bars federal contractors or subcontractors from employment discrimination on the basis of disability.	No effect found.

1976	In *Planned Parenthood of Central Missouri v. Danforth*, the court struck down state laws requiring the consent of spouses and parents of patients under the age of 18 before an abortion procedure. It ruled the Missouri laws unconstitutional because they "delegated to third parties an absolute veto power which the state does not itself possess."	No effect found.
1978	In *Regents of the University of California v. Bakke*, the Supreme Court ruled that the medical school's special admission program setting aside a fixed number of seats for minorities violated Title VI of the 1964 Civil Rights Act. At the same time, however, in an opinion written by Justice Powell, it ruled that race could lawfully be considered as one of several factors in making admissions decisions. Justice Powell noted that lawful affirmative action programs may be based on reasons other than redressing past discrimination, in particular, a university's educational interest in attaining a diverse student body could justify appropriate affirmative action programs.	No effect found.
1987	In *United States v. Paradise*, the Supreme Court upheld a one-for-one promotion requirement—i.e., for every white candidate promoted, a qualified African American would also be promoted—in the Alabama Department of Public Safety.	No effect found.
1988	**Fair Housing Amendments Act** - disabled access required for multi-family housing intended for first occupancy after 13 March 1991.	No effect expected, no effect found.
1989	**Air Carriers Access Act** - disabled access required in construction of terminal facilities owned or operated by an air carrier.	No effect expected, no effect found.
1990	**Americans with Disabilities Act** - Title I prohibits disability discrimination by employers. Titles II and III require disability access in all places of public accommodation and business for first occupancy after 26 January 1993 or for occupancy for new alterations, and in all state and local government facilities, after 26 January 1992.	No effect expected: mild increase from previous year.
1989-1992	Series of Pro-Life Supreme Court Decisions (*Webster v. Reproductive Health Services, Rust v. Sullivan, and Planned Parenthood v. Casey*) in which state laws regarding provision of increased state supervision of abortion procedures were upheld.	Increase in number of attacks, especially abortion-related attacks.

1991	**Civil Rights Act** - adds provisions to Title VII protections, including right to jury trial.	No effect expected, no effect found.
1993-4	**Brady Handgun Violence Prevention Act** – institutes a federal background check on firearms purchases in the United States	Increase in the level of violence starting in 1994; rise of the militia movement
1993-4	**Violent Crime Control and Law Enforcement Act** – prevented purchases of specific firearms with specific characteristics	Increase in the level of violence starting in 1994; rise of the militia movement
2010	In *McDonald v. Chicago* the Court held that the right of an individual to "keep and bear arms" protected by the Second Amendment is incorporated by the Due Process Clause of the Fourteenth Amendment and applies to the states. This resolved the uncertainty left in the wake of *District of Columbia v. Heller* as to the scope of gun rights in regard to the states.	No effect expected, decrease in the level of violence.

Table 1 provides several insights into the dynamic of far-right violence. First, three clusters of events facilitated its rise: the Supreme Court decisions against segregation in the education system; the Civil Rights Acts of 1964 and the anti-gun legislation of 1993—1994. Most of the other pieces of legislation focused mainly on disability rights and affirmative action, and therefore had a limited impact on trends of far-right violence. It appears that when legislation directly impacts on individual daily practices, some groups from within the affected communities will tend to react, resorting to violent measures. Second, in all cases there was a vociferous local leadership which framed the legislation as almost an "existential threat" to the community's way of life. Both aspects—catastrophic framing by leadership and challenging policies—correspond with findings of previous studies which analyzed political violence within counterculture communities.

Another interesting insight is the linkage between the level of violence and Supreme Court decisions on abortion issues. The initial Supreme Court decisions which set the legal foundations for the legality of abortion procedures in the United States during the 1970s met with a limited response from the far right, i.e., no abortion-related attacks could be identified during 1973–1976, and in general these years were characterized by limited violence. However, a series of pro-life decisions in 1989 and the early 1990s facilitated a significant rise in far-right violence, in particular in abortion-related attacks. To illustrate, while in 1988/89 there were seven and eight abortion-related attacks respectively, during 1990–1992 no less than 75 attacks on abortion-related targets were documented. These findings generally correspond with the results presented earlier, i.e., far right groups and individuals appear to be empowered by what could be perceived as growing support for their values within the political and judicial systems. While the theoretical implications of these findings will be considered later, we can summarize by stating that far right violence usually increases in a contentious political environment when this environment tends to conservatism. However, sparks of violence can also be triggered regardless, in times of direct or perceived threat to a distinct ideological grouping's normative practices. But are these processes more prevalent in specific geographical areas? The next section addresses this question.

4.2.2 – The Evolution of the American Far-Right Violence: Geographical Context

The significant social and demographic differences between regions in the United States make the country a convenient laboratory for evaluating how geographic and demographic characteristics articulate with the level and nature of far-right violence.

Table 2 reflects the distribution of attacks since 1990 among the different US states and other theoretically relevant state characteristics.[359] These include: population size and population density—which serve mainly as control variables, as it may be assumed that the greater the population, the higher the chances for the existence of social outliers or radicals willing to engage in violent action, or that the more dense the population is, interaction between social outliers or radicals and potential target communities is more likely; and the size and portion of the overall population of three major minority groups which are targeted by far-right groups. Finally, the overall proportion of the entire minorities population is also included.

---

[359] While state level analyses are not rare within the realm of American far right studies: see e.g., Van Dyke and Soule, 497–520; Freilich. The findings require further evaluation with county-level analyses to negate the possibility of ecological fallacy.

Table 2 – Far-Right Violence and Demographic Variables by State[123]

State	Attacks	Population	AM (African American) Population	Proportion of AM population (%)	Hispanic Population	Proportion of Hispanic population (%)	Jewish Population	Proportion of Jewish population (%)	Population density	Proportion of Minorities
1. California	782	37,691,912	2,299,072	6.67	13,434,896	36.6	1,219,740	3.3	241.7	59.9
2. New York	494	19,465,197	3,073,800	15.18	3,232,360	16.6	1,635,020	8.4	412.3	41.7
3. Florida	245	19,057,542	2,999,862	15.91	3,846,267	21	638,635	3.4	353.4	42.1
4. Texas	186	25,674,681	2,979,598	11.91	8,815,582	36.2	139,565	0.6	98.07	44.7
5. Illinois	172	12,869,257	1,866,414	14.88	1,961,843	15.2	297,935	2.3	231.5	36.3
6. Massachusetts	157	6,587,536	434,398	7.02	556,573	8.6	277,980	4.2	840.2	23.9
7. Pennsylvania	157	12,742,886	1,377,689	10.79	588,950	4.7	294,925	2.3	284.3	20.5
8. Washington	144	6,830,038	240,042	3.74	642,959	9.8	45,885	0.7	102.6	27.5
9. New Jersey	138	8,821,155	1,204,826	14.46	1,424,069	16.4	504,450	5.7	1189	40.7
10. Oregon	126	3,871,859	69,206	2.01	417,152	11	40,650	1.1	40.33	21.5
11. Maryland	98	5,828,289	1,700,298	29.44	372,650	6.6	238,000	4.1	596.3	45.3
12. Arizona	93	6,482,505	259,008	4.16	1,964,625	30.2	106,400	1.7	57	42.23
13. North Carolina	85	9,656,401	2,048,628	21.6	678,023	7.4	30,675	0.3	198.2	34.7
14. Wisconsin	79	5,711,767	359,148	6.07	286,382	5.1	28,255	0.5	105.2	16.7
15. Indiana	76	6,516,922	591,397	9.07	322,148	5.1	17,470	0.3	181.7	18.5
16. Ohio	73	11,544,951	1,407,681	12.04	296,059	2.6	148,380	1.3	281.9	18.9
17. Virginia	71	8,096,604	1,551,399	19.91	528,002	6.8	97,290	1.2	204.5	35.2
18. Michigan	70	9,876,187	1,400,362	14.24	408,695	4.1	82,270	0.8	173.9	23.4
19. Connecticut	69	3,580,709	362,296	10.34	424,191	12.1	116,050	3.2	739.1	18.8
20. Colorado	68	5,116,769	201,737	4.28	993,198	20.1	91,070	1.8	49.33	30
21. Missouri	67	6,010,688	704,043	11.49	182,059	3.1	59,175	1	87.26	19
22. Louisiana	65	4,574,836	1,452,396	31.98	152,781	3.5	10,675	0.2	105	39.7
23. Georgia	63	9,815,210	2,950,435	30.02	780,408	8.1	127,670	1.3	169.5	44.1
24. Minnesota	63	5,344,861	274,412	4.57	217,551	4.2	45,635	0.9	67.14	16.9
25. Tennessee	59	6,403,353	1,055,689	16.78	234,868	3.8	19,600	0.3	155.4	24.4
26. Iowa	45	3,062,309	89,148	2.68	124,030	4.1	6,240	0.2	54.81	11.3
27. DC	43	617,996	313,000	50.7	51,260	8.7	28,000	4.7	10065	65.2
28. South Carolina	43	4,679,230	1,290,684	28.48	177,999	4	12,545	0.3	155.4	35.9
29. Kentucky	41	4,369,356	337,520	7.71	100,366	2.4	11,300	0.3	110	13.7
30. Nevada	41	2,723,322	218,626	8.1	672,393	25.9	74,400	2.8	24.8	45.9
31. Maine	35	1,328,188	15,707	1.03	12,700	1	13,890	1	43.04	5.6
32. Utah	35	2,817,222	29,287	1.27	323,938	11.8	5,650	0.2	34.3	19.6
33. Alabama	32	4,802,740	1,251,311	26.38	128,586	2.8	8,850	0.2	94.65	33
34. Idaho	32	1,584,985	9,810	0.95	159,257	10.5	1,525	0.1	19.15	16
35. Oklahoma	30	3,791,508	277,644	7.96	278,676	7.7	4,700	0.1	55.02	21.3
36. New Hampshire	29	1,318,194	15,035	1.22	39,123	3	10,120	0.8	147	7.7
37. New Mexico	29	2,082,224	42,550	2.97	895,150	45.1	12,175	0.6	17.16	59.5
38. Arkansas	26	2,937,979	449,895	15.76	155,309	5.4	1,725	0.1	56.43	25.5
39. Kansas	23	2,871,238	167,864	6.15	268,964	9.6	17,775	0.6	35.09	21.8
40. West Virginia	21	1,855,364	63,124	3.58	21,400	1.2	2,335	0.1	77.06	6.8
41. Mississippi	20	2,978,512	1,098,385	37.18	56,632	1.9	1,575	0.1	63.5	42
42. Montana	20	998,199	4,027	0.67	31,093	3.2	1,350	0.1	6.8	12.2
43. Nebraska	19	1,842,641	82,885	4.5	147,968	8.3	6,100	0.3	23.97	17.9
44. Rhode Island	16	1,051,302	60,189	6.36	120,662	11.5	18,750	1.8	1006	23.6
45. Vermont	15	626,431	6,277	0.87	6,651	1.1	5,385	0.9	67.73	5.7
46. Delaware	13	907,135	191,814	20.95	62,506	7.2	15,100	1.7	464.3	34.7
47. South Dakota	9	824,082	10,207	1.14	22,420	2.8	395	0	10.86	15.3
48. Alaska	8	722,718	23,263	4.27	37,420	5.5	6,150	0.9	1.2	35.9
49. North Dakota	8	683,932	7,960	1.08	13,634	2.1	400	0.1	9.9	11.1
50. Wyoming	6	568,158	4,748	1.29	43,385	8.1	950	0.2	5.8	14.1
51. Hawaii	3	1,374,810	21,424	3.08	108,663	8.4	7,280	0.5	214.1	77.3

[1] State's data is based on 2010 general census.

[2] While demographic changes occur over time, several factors limit the impact of these in the current analysis. First, the relatively short time-frame analyzed; second, the majority of the violence occurring in the last decade, thus limiting further possible distortion in the findings; finally, the growth of a number of minority groups, which accords with overall population growth (African American, Jewish).

The findings provide several important insights regarding the dynamics and geographical dispersion of far-right violence and challenge conventional wisdom. To begin with, the area which was the birthplace of groups such as the KKK and the major concentration of far right violence during the 1960s, is no longer the natural habitat of the violent American far right. North Carolina, the southern state with the highest level of far-right violence, is ranked only thirteenth among all states. If we include Texas, we can only find two southern states in the top 15. Furthermore, the states which were mostly associated with the American far-right in the past are mostly ranked in the middle or the lower third in terms of number of attacks, including Mississippi (ranked 41), West Virginia (40), Kansas (39), Alabama (33), Kentucky (29), South Carolina (28), Tennessee (25), Georgia (23), Louisiana (22) and Missouri (21). This clearly represents a different situation than forty or fifty years ago, when the Deep South was engraved in the American collective mindset as a hotbed of racial, anti-abortion and religiously driven violence.

If the South is no longer the hub of far right violence, which regions are? It appears that the exact opposite is the case. In terms of the number of attacks, the two states at the top of the list are California and New York, which are considered liberal—or blue—in terms of their ideological and political orientation. To illustrate, both states have voted for Democratic presidential candidates in the last 24 years. When looking at the rest of the states that occupy the top ten spots, the blue trend is consistent: we can find Illinois (ranked 5th), Massachusetts (6th), Pennsylvania (7th), Washington (8th), New Jersey (9th) and Oregon (10th). Thus, it can be determined that during the last twenty years the violence has shifted from the center/South to the coasts and the North (with the exception of Texas).

The existence of significant minority groups in the different states appears linked with the level of far-right violence they experience. The table indicates that the top four states in terms of number of attacks also have the highest number of combined African American and Hispanic residents. Moreover, eight of the top ten states in terms of the number of Jewish residents are also in the top ten in terms of number of attacks. Nevertheless, despite these initial findings, more systematic and rigorous procedures are needed in order to evaluate the relationship between the trends in far-right violence and geographical and demographic characteristics. Basic analysis shows strong and statistically significant correlation between the number of attacks per state and African American population size ($\alpha=.598^{***}$); Hispanic population size ($\alpha=.849^{***}$) and proportion ($\alpha=.492^{***}$); and size ($\alpha=.900^{***}$) and proportion ($\alpha=.575^{***}$) of Jewish population. Finally, the overall number of minorities in general is also positively correlated with the number of attacks (α=.344*).

While these findings may be persuasive, the strong correlation between the level of violence and state population size (α=.888**) requires us to resort to a procedure which will evaluate the above findings when controlling for potential intervening variables. Two-stage hierarchical regression analysis—intended for controlling both state population size and density—was performed (the change in R^2 was .179***). The analysis exposes a nuanced picture regarding the relations between the level of violence and in-state size and proportion of minority groups. While both the size and proportion of the African American population (β=.47*** and β=.16** respectively) and the size (β=.69***) and proportion (β=.11)[360] of Jewish population remained statistically significantly congruent with the level of violence, this is not the case with the size or proportion of the Hispanic population. While the meaning of these findings will be discussed later in this study, it appears that anti-Semitic and anti-African American sentiments and narratives are still emphasized and dominant within the ideological frameworks of most far-right streams; and a potential identification problem exists, i.e., African American and Jewish organizational frameworks are more visible, hence there is a delay in the identification of the Hispanic minority as a threat by far-right groups.

4.2.3 – The Development of American Far-Right Violence: Socio-Economic Context

The political violence literature is rich in theoretical frameworks associating political violence with economic conditions: many scholars have assumed that most individuals who join violent sub-state groups are suffering from frustration and desperation which, in most cases, is a result of humiliation and perceived economic deprivation.[361] In the case of the American far-right, the emergence of at least some of its streams has traditionally been seen as a result of socio-economic crisis, e.g., the rise of the militia movement following the 1980s farm crisis and the rise of the Skinheads following the decline of inner-cities regions in the mid to late 1980s. While these linkages may be valid, at least when looking at the overall extent of American far right violence, economic indicators have limited capacity to explain trends in the violence.

---

[360] In this specific finding, P<.063.

[361] See - Piazza. A. James, "Rooted in Poverty?: Terrorism, Poor Economic Development, and Social Cleavages," *Terrorism and Political Violence*, 18 (2006), 159–177.

Figure 3 – Domestic Economic Indicators between 1954-2011

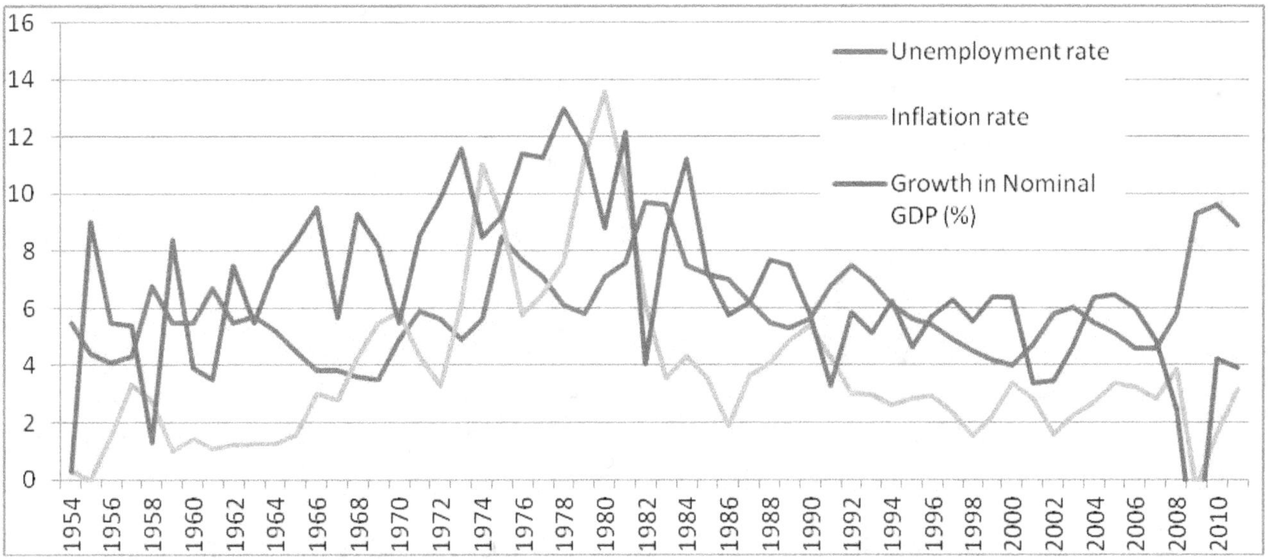

Several pro-cyclic indicators are commonly used in order to measure the economic health of a polity; among them are the unemployment rate, gross domestic product (GDP) and inflation rate. These three indicators' yearly values between 1954 and 2011 are represented in Figure 3. When compared with yearly numbers of attacks, two negative correlations are found to be statistically significant: inflation rate (α=-.277*) and nominal GDP growth (α=-.486***). While the former corresponds with the abovementioned deprivation thesis, the latter does not. When multivariate analysis was performed, only nominal GDP growth remained significant. The insignificance of the factors which normally more directly impact individuals' quality of life, the lack of supporting evidence—e.g., it seems that the more economically developed states are more vulnerable to far-right violence—and the lack of individual-level data, demand caution when trying to explain far-right violence by means of socio-economic causes.

4. 3 – The Evolution of American Far-Right Violence: Operational Context

Before considering the theoretical and analytical implications of the findings presented above, an overview of the operational characteristics of the violence produced by the American far right is required. This will help to evaluate aspects related to its productivity, effectiveness and overall operational capabilities, and to how these are related to its ability to impact social and political processes. Hence, the following section will cover aspects of far-right violence related to the level of violence, in terms of casualties, tactical tendencies and target selection.

Figure 4 – Number of Victims per Year, 1990–2011

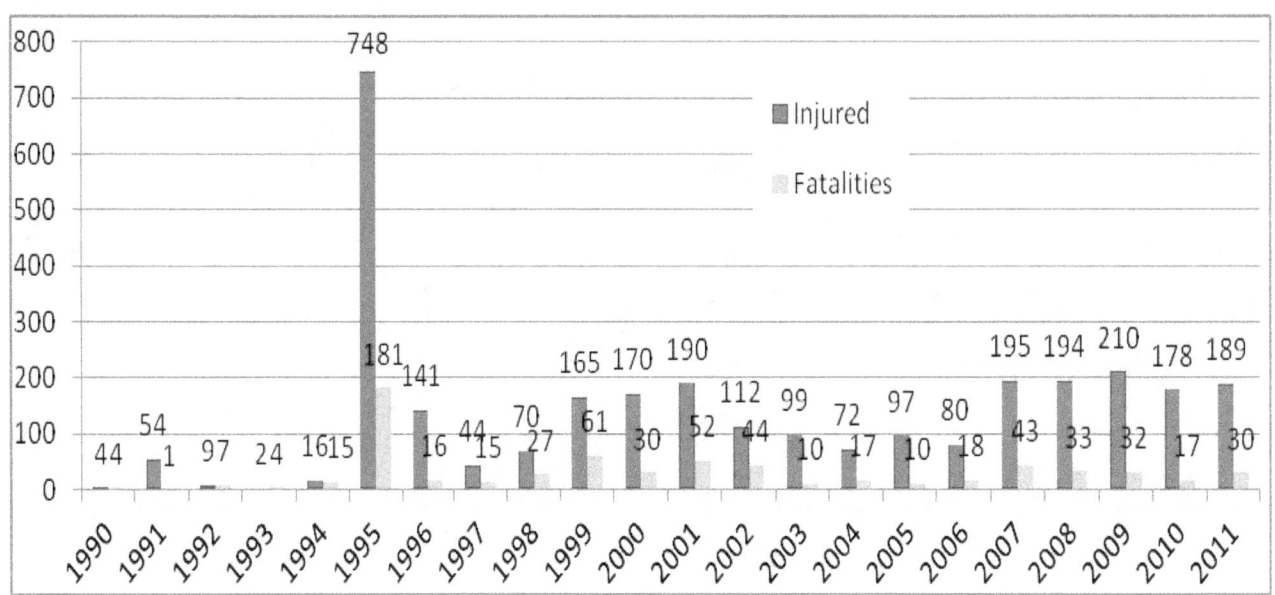

Figure 4A – Number of Victims per Year, 1990–2011(Higher Resolution)

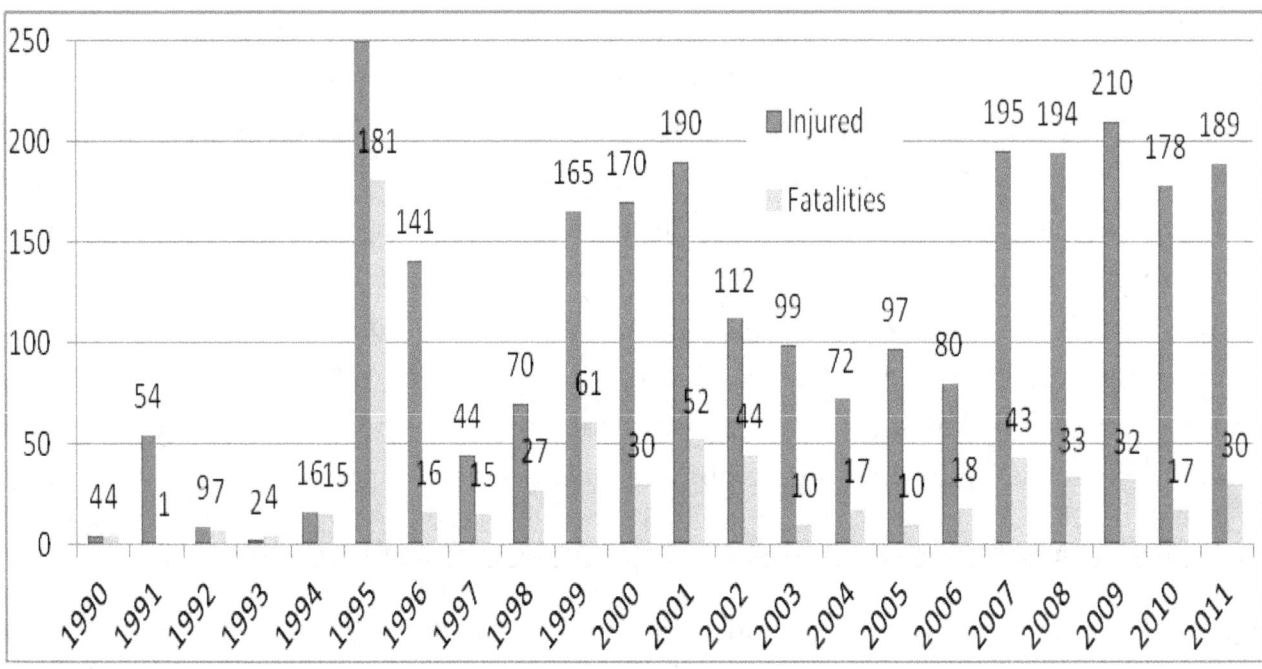

One of the popular parameters employed by students of terrorism for assessing the effectiveness and the impact of terrorist campaigns are the number of victims they generate.[362] The rationale is that the psychological and symbolic impact of terrorist

---

[362] See e.g., James A. Piazza, "Rooted in Poverty?: Terrorism, Poor Economic Development, and Social Cleavages," *Terrorism and Political Violence*, 18 (2006), 159–77.

attacks—the main factors by which terrorism seeks to facilitate political change—are closely linked to the number of individuals who were victimized. In the context of the American far-right, the relevant numbers are presented in Figures 4 and 4A.

With the exception of 1995's OKBOMB casualties, it can be seen that the last decade has been more lethal than the 1990s, a trend that corresponds with the increase in the number of attacks during the 2000s. A more nuanced interpretation allows us to identify four distinct phases. The first, between 1990 and 1998, is characterized by a relatively low number of fatalities and injuries, subject again to the exception of 1995. Between 1999 and 2002 we can see a significant rise in the casualty rates attributable to far-right violence as the number of injured rose to over 100, and except for 2002, over 150. The number of fatalities was usually a few dozen. Between 2003 and 2006 there is a decline in casualties, as in those years the number of victims declines below 100 injured and 20 fatalities. Finally, between 2007 and 2011 there is again a rise in the number of victims, to the highest levels documented so far.

Although providing some idea regarding the highs and lows of far-right violence in terms of the number of victims it has generated, the above numbers still cannot enable an accurate assessment of its productivity in this regard. This term refers to the ability to maximize the number of victims for each violent operation. Thus, in order to assess productivity we need to calculate the average number of victims per attack while controlling for attacks which initially were not intended to result in human casualties or were not capable of doing so, i.e., attacks against property, or attacks that were not completed.

Figure 5 – Average Number of Victims per Event on Yearly Basis, 1990–2012

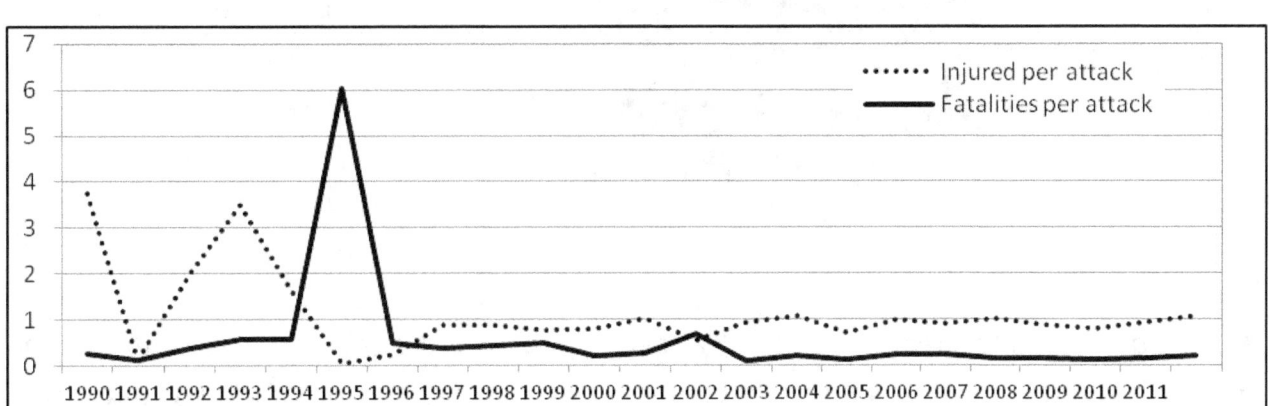

Figure 5 provides the results of these procedures by illustrating the average number of victims per attack on an annual basis. As can be seen, the picture is significantly different from the one presented in Figure 4. Whereas during the 2000s there is an increase in the number of victims as a result of the rise in the number of attacks, in terms of productivity of the attacks, there are no significant changes in the last 15 years. In other words, we cannot argue that far-right violence has become more sophisticated or effective in increasing the number of victims caused by its violent activities.

This is an intriguing finding, especially when considering that what is termed the "new terrorism" of the last 30 years is characterized by significant operational advances.[363] Hence, in periods during which many streams of terrorism have shown improvement in their operational capabilities and, as a result, an increase in their tendency to engage in mass casualty attacks, the violent American far right shows stagnation, at least in terms of its ability to enhance the harm it generates.

In order to further our understanding of the American far-right lack of operational development, a more in-depth look at its operational characteristics is needed. Figure 6 presents the distribution of far right attacks based on types of attacks.

Figure 6 – American Far Right Violence by Type of Attack, 1990–2012

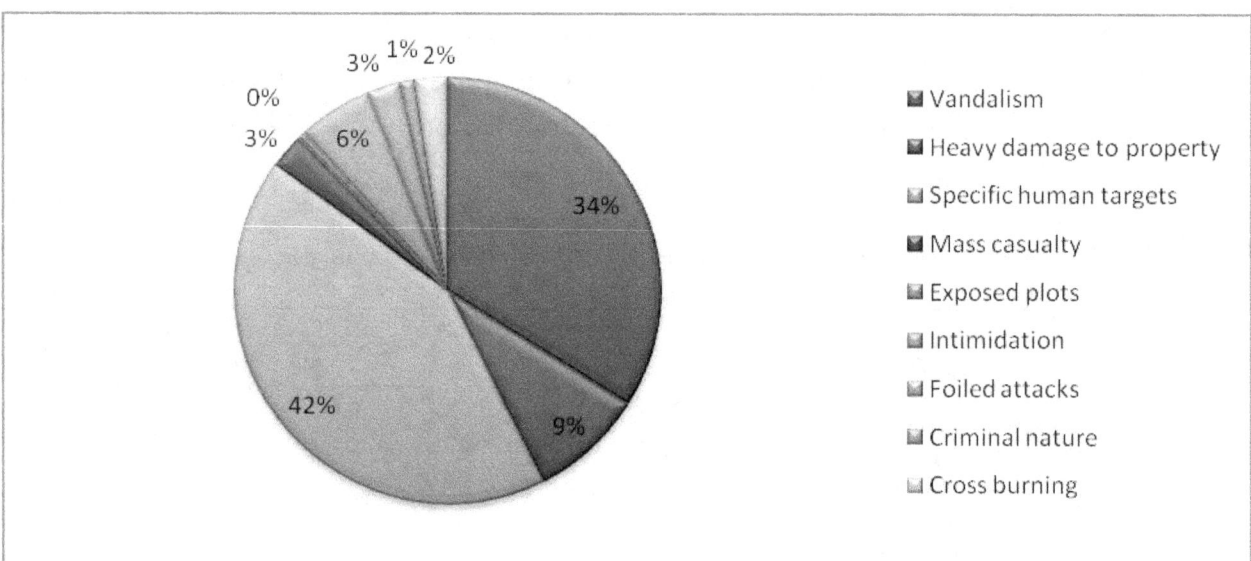

As can be seen, the great majority of attacks are directed against property (43%) and specific human targets (42%). Just three percent of the attacks were intended to cause—

---

[363] David Tucker, "What is new about the new terrorism," *Terrorism and Political Violence,* 13 (2001), 1–14.

or were successful in generating—mass casualty incidents,[364] further emphasizing the difficulty of far right violence to make the leap from small-scale attacks against specific human targets to large-scale activities of indiscriminate violence that have the potential to generate a high number of casualties.

The findings presented in Figure 6 may also imply that the operational-social framework of the violent American far right could be better understood—with some modifications—via the framework of the iceberg theory "...of political extremism of social/political movements," originally developed by Sprinzak almost 40 years ago.[365] In the context of the American far right, it seems that we have a large base of supporters— the base of the iceberg—who are usually engaged in low-level violence such as minor incidents of vandalism or low-sophistication attacks against individuals.[366] The tip of the iceberg includes a relatively small number of people who are responsible for producing mass-casualty attacks. Further developing the analogy, we can say that most of the low-level attacks have received relatively little attention from the media, political authorities and law enforcement: this is the submerged part of the iceberg which cannot be seen. The few mass-casualty attacks, represented by the visible tip of the iceberg, attract most of the attention.

Nevertheless, the common wisdom is that the most damaging and dangerous mass of the iceberg is the proportionally larger submerged segment, hence the high volume of violence which is reflected in vandalism and specific attacks against individuals. This model offers a more precise indication of the growing threat from the far right than the small number of mass-casualty attacks. This is particularly true when considering that rarely will a group or individual engage in mass-casualty attacks without engaging first

---

[364] Indiscriminate attacks which includes tactics aiming to maximize the number of casualties (i.e. car-bomb, shooting with automatic rifle into crowded area etc.).

[365] In the early 1980s the Israeli political scientist Ehud Sprinzak published a paper on the irredentist Israeli religio-political movement *Gush Emunim* ("The Bloc of the Faithful") entitled "The Iceberg Model of Political Extremism." In it he argued that the *Gush* is best understood not as a classical protest movement, but as the extremist tip of a large social and cultural "iceberg," in effect a religious subculture, which supports and nurtures the *Gush*. Pyramidal in structure, this iceberg—*Gush's* social and political basis of support—broadens as one moves from the politically extremist tip to the non-extremist base. See Ehud Sprinzak, "Gush Emunim, the Iceberg Model of Political Extremism," *Medina, Mimshal Veyahasim Beinleumiim*, 17 (1981) (Hebrew).

[366] Blee uses the concept of "narrative racial terrorism" to describe these types of attacks. She explains that these attacks are "somewhat spontaneous, in which victims are chosen impulsively and without clear purpose, and whose consequences are rarely calculated by the perpetrators in advance." See Blee.

in low profile attacks.[367] Therefore, it is possible that growth of the base of the iceberg will eventually also be reflected in an increase in the stability and extent of the visible tip, indicative of greater numbers of mass-casualty attacks.

Figure 7 – American Far Right Violence by Type of Targets, 1990–2012

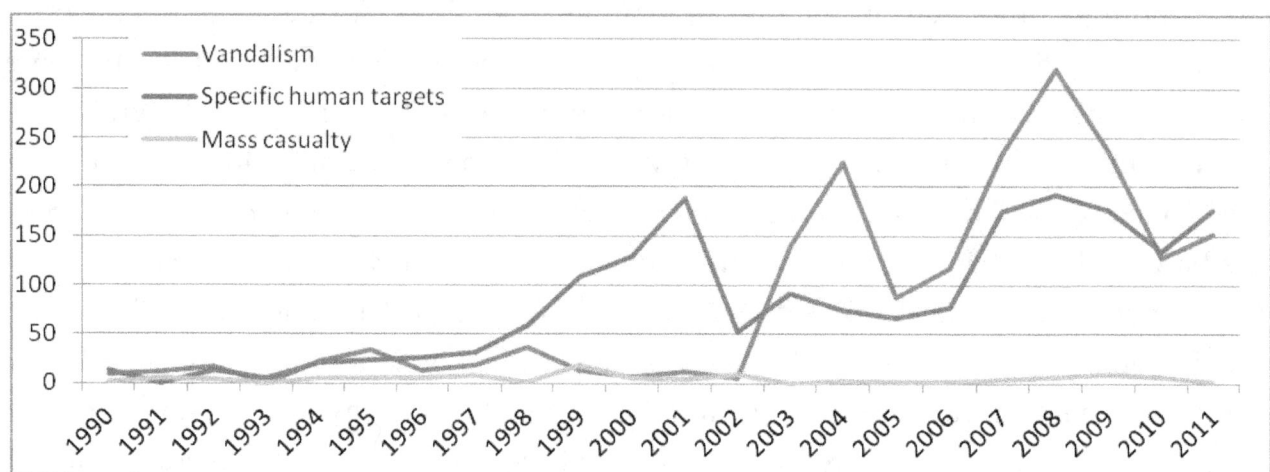

To conclude, if this perspective is a reflection of the movement's structure and dynamics, then we may be facing a continuous rise in the level of violence since—as can be seen in Figure 7—the last six years have been characterized by an overall increase in the base of the iceberg, which is followed by a concomitant increase in the number of mass-casualty attacks; this trend is also visible during 1999–2000, with a rise in the number of low-level attacks being followed by an increase in mass-casualty attacks.

The applicability of the iceberg model to American far-right violence is also supported by the specific weapons and tactics used.

---

[367] For example, in their research on Jewish terrorist groups, Pedahzur and Perliger showed that most members of the terrorist groups were involved in minor incidents prior to engagement in more systematic campaigns of violence. See Ami Pedahzur and Arie Perliger, *Jewish Terrorism in Israel* (New York: Columbia University Press, 2009).

Figure 8 – American Far Right Violence by Type of Weapon,1990–2012

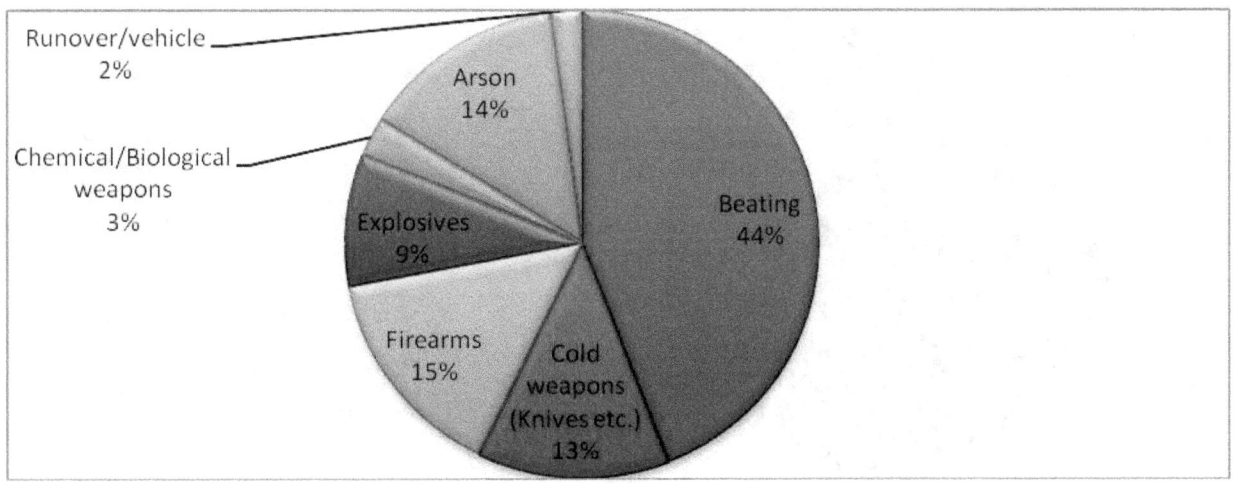

As shown in Figure 8, a clear hierarchy of sophistication exists, with beating and cold weapons constituting the majority of the attacks (57%), while more sophisticated weapons such as firearms and explosives constitute a second degree of sophistication, i.e., 24% of the attacks, while arson is a unique category since, in many cases, it is aimed against property and not people. On a side note, notwithstanding their limited level of sophistication, far right elements have been using chemical and biological weapons in a considerable number of cases. While most of these attacks were not sophisticated in their execution, such as contaminating the medical equipment of abortion clinics with chemical materials, they still indicate a degree of innovation.

The last operational dimension which will be analyzed is target selection (see Figure 9), which could be explained by re-addressing the conceptualization of the far right as it was presented in the first part of this study. As can be seen in Figure 9, 65% of the attacks were directed against various minorities, including attacks against educational and religious institutions affiliated with minority groups. This could be explained both on an ideological-symbolic level and by more practical-operational considerations. From an ideological-symbolic perspective, the core components of the far right ideology—internal homogeneity and nativism—and other commonly shared ideological components—xenophobia, racism and exclusionism—refer to practices that aim to shape the boundaries between, and more precisely define, the ostracized and the elect. Therefore it is not surprising that outsiders are the main targets of far-right groups and individuals.

Figure 9 – American Far Right Violence by Type of Targets, 1990–2012

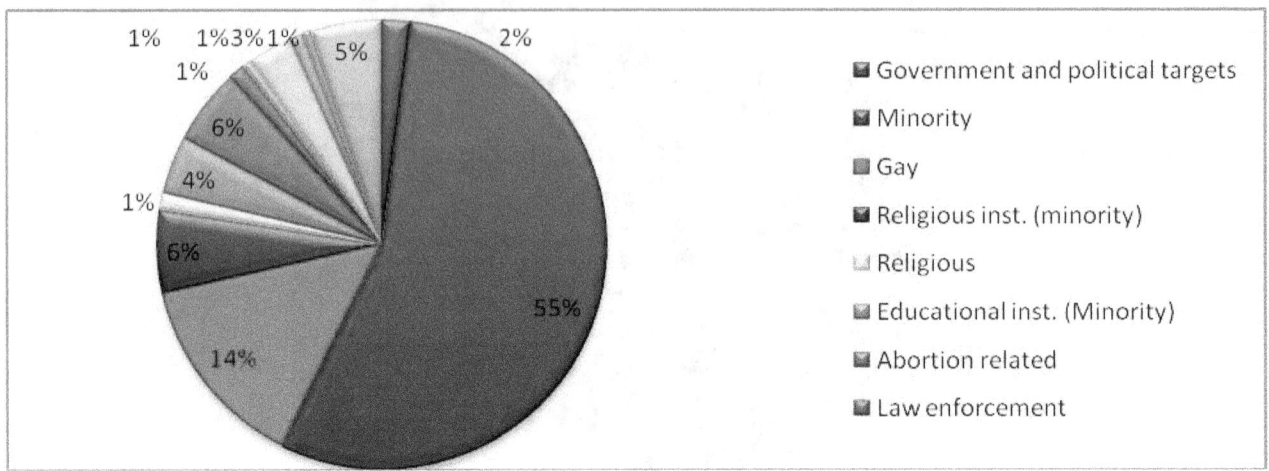

Moreover, attacking outsiders also serves a symbolic signaling purpose. The literature regards terrorist attacks as symbolic violence that is used to communicate a political message aiming at challenging the hegemonic construction of political reality.[368] A symbol is "an object or a phenomenon used to provide a meaning not inherent in the object itself."[369] In the case of terrorism, we are dealing with a violent act whose different components, i.e., the characteristics of the act, such as targets selected, tactics used, and timing, are used to convey a message to different audiences in order to impact the perception of reality and one's place in it.[370] In the case of the American far right, violence is practiced in order to prevent the further blurring of the boundaries between "Americans" and "non-Americans" by communicating a clear message of who constitutes legitimate members of the collective and the nation. This rationale also helps to explain the positive correlation between the size and proportion of minority populations in a specific state, and the level of violence in that state, since it is precisely in these types of states—with high proportions of minorities—that higher chances exist for ambiguity regarding the definition of "outsiders" and "insiders," and concomitantly a broader pool of available targets.

From a practical-operational perspective, some immigrant and minority communities, with a recent history in the United States, typically constitute a more vulnerable part of

---

[368] Martha Crenshaw, "Causes of Terrorism," *Comparative Politics* 13(4) (1981), 379–99.
[369] R. W. Cobb and M. H. Ross, "Agenda Setting and the Denial of Agenda Access: Key Concepts" in ed. R. W. Cobb and M. H. Ross, *Cultural Strategies of Agenda Denial* (Lawrence: University Press of Kansas, 1997).
[370] See e.g., Schmid and Jongman, 7.

society: they have limited access to political power and economic resources and, as a result, are unable to secure severe sanctions against those threatening them; they are easy to identify and are likely to have contentious relations with law enforcement agencies. Thus, it is easy to understand why far-right elements might assume that attacking minorities will have limited potential costs in comparison to the costs of attacking other types of targets.

Several further insights regarding target selection are worth mentioning. To begin with, some of the targets appear to be related to specific ideological movements. For instance, attacks against law enforcement and government institutions correlate with the anti-federalist movement, while abortion-related targets are associated with the fundamentalist movement. This probable link between specific ideological tendencies and operational characteristics will be examined more closely in later sections of this study. Second, individuals and groups related to alternative sexual orientations surprisingly constitute a large proportion of the targets chosen by far right elements. The fact that the proclivity to attack these kinds of targets is a recent trend—more than 50% of the attacks have occurred in the last five years and more than two thirds in the last decade—may imply that we are seeing a counter-response to the growing political and legal success of groups from the left of the political spectrum promoting civil rights in the context of sexual preference, e.g., the expansion of legislation allowing same-sex marriage, while DC, Hawaii and California were the only states/districts which allowed same sex partnerships before 2000. Since 2000, 13 other states have passed such legislation.

Finally, attacks against perceived enemies from within—i.e., political competitors such as left-wing or liberal political elements—is a trend which is visible in other similar arenas of far-right violence, but which is not discernible in the American case. How can this be explained? Is it merely because attacking such targets is more problematic or less effective in framing the message far right groups are interested in conveying? Or is it a result of identification problems and limited operational accessibility? These targets are naturally not highly visible, nor are they accessible or identifiable as viable targets: are the costs involved in acquiring the comprehension regarding the nature of the specific organization, and of the process of framing it as a viable target, higher than those related to obvious targets such as minority facilities? The next section, which is devoted to placing the empirical findings presented above in a theoretical and analytical context, will help to answer these questions, and provide a better understanding of the trends within the American far right.

4.4 – Theoretical and Analytical Implications

In order to comprehend how the findings presented above promote our understanding of the causes and characteristics of far-right violence, we must first delve into—and provide a basic introduction to—two spheres of literature. The first deals with the causes of political violence; the second focuses on the factors which facilitate popular support for, and political activism in, far-right groups/movements. While in both cases the scope of this study does not allow for a full literature review, it is still important to provide a basic overview of the major theoretical approaches.

4.4.1 – Theories of Political Violence

The first academic investigations of political violence, especially of terrorist/sub-state groups, appeared in the early 1960s. Since then, great efforts have been made by scholars from different branches of the social sciences to decipher the processes and motives that impel individuals to take part in acts of political violence. The different approaches can be classified in accordance with their sphere of research and its relation to the perpetrator of violence. Thus, alongside studies which focus on the individual, we can find studies which focus on their interaction/socialization with family members, peers and a close social environment, as well as studies which analyze the characteristics of the individual's cultural or political community.

The first scholars to study sub-state political violence were perplexed by the willingness of individuals to sacrifice personal resources and partake in risky and life-threatening activities for the sake of what they perceived as altruistic goals.[371] This perspective, combined with the observation that terrorists are inclined to engage in especially cruel manifestations of violence, fostered the popularity of two perceptions regarding the nature of terrorists/perpetrators. The first was partially based on Freudian theories, which link frustration and violence,[372] and it assumed that terrorists are individuals suffering from frustration and desperation, which in most cases is a result of past

---

[371] D. G. Hubbard, *The skyjacker: His flights of fantasy* (New York: Macmillan, 1971); F. J. Hacker, *Crusaders, criminals, crazies: Terror and terrorism in our time* (New York: Norton, 1976).

[372] J. Dollard, L. W. Doob, N. E. Miller, W. Mowrer, and R. R. Sears, *Frustration and Aggression* (New Haven, Connecticut: Yale University Press, 1939); Schmid and Jongman, 7.

humiliation and perceived economic deprivation; hence frustration, and the view that terrorism was the only alternative to achieve meaningful lives, drove these individuals to engage in political violence. This perspective gradually met growing criticism as studies showed that the linkage between frustration and violence is doubtful.[373] Furthermore, studies demonstrated that in reality a large majority of the terrorists originate from affluent classes of society.[374] The second perspective was that terrorists share some common psychopathologies. Whereas some scholars expected to find that terrorists suffer from major mental clinical illnesses, others assumed that terrorists suffer from personality disorders, especially sociopathic personalities.[375] Among the popular traits mentioned in this body of literature were narcissistic tendencies, unconsolidated personality, low self-esteem and unformed self-identity. A branch of this psychological-individual approach also sought to understand the mental conditions of the terrorists by looking at their childhood socialization. While some of them emphasized a combination of non-functioning and underachieving parents with problematic personality traits,[376] others claimed that individuals whose parents had high political awareness and/or who were oppressed by the state because of their political activism, would be highly motivated to engage in terrorism to avenge the oppression of his/her parents and to continue their political struggle.[377] Notwithstanding, from the mid-1980s, a growing number of scholars have suggested that the most common trait among terrorists is normalcy. Indeed, the pathological theoretical approach has never received substantial empirical support.[378]

---

[373] R. J. Rummel, *Field Theory Evolving* (Beverly Hills, California: Sage Publications, 1977).

[374] See for example Alan B. Kruger and Jitka Maleckova, "Education, Poverty and Terrorism," *Journal of Economic Perspectives* (17), 4 (2003), 119–44.

[375] Jeff Victoroff, "The Mind of the Terrorist: A Review and Critique of Psychological Approaches," *Journal of Conflict Resolution*, 49(1) (2005), 3–42.

[376] Hubbard.

[377] V. D. Volkan, *Blood Lines: Fromethnic Pride to Ethnic Terrorism* (New York : Farrar, Straus,&Giroux, 1997); Jessica Stern, *Terror in the name of God: Why religious militants kill* (New York: Ecco, 2003); K. Kellen, "Ideology and Rebellion: Terrorism in West Germany," in Walter Reich ed. *The Origins of Terrorism* (Washington: Woodrow Wilson Center Press, 1990), 43–58.

[378] Walter Reich, "Understanding Terrorist Behavior: The Limits and Opportunities of Psychological Inquiry," in Walter Reich ed. *Origins of Terrorism: Psychologies, Ideologies, Theologies, States of mind*, Washington, DC: Woodrow Wilson Center Press, 1998), 261–79; Andrew P. Silke, "Cheshire-cat Logic: The Recurring Theme of Terrorist Abnormality in Psychological Research," *Psychology, Crime and Law* 4 (1998), 51–69; John Horgan, "The Search for the Terrorist Personality," in ed. Andrew Silke *Terrorists, Victims and Society* (Chichester, UK: Wiley, 2003) 3–27.

Studies which emphasized social learning processes paved the way for scholars who claimed that the dynamic within the terrorist's social networks are sometimes more responsible for the inclination to engage in violence than ideological affinities or personality traits.[379] By analyzing the social ties of the terrorists, and the structure and characteristics of the social network of terrorist groups, these studies aim to portray the paths of how groups and individuals slide into violence. Generally, they have argued that most terrorist incidents are a product of a social network which operates within social enclaves alienated from society and from mainstream culture and which radicalize in times of external threats to their values. The members' conformity with the social network's values is expressed by participating in political violence.[380]

The "social network studies" did not simply undermine the importance of psychological explanations but were also a counter-response, in some degree, to the influx of studies focusing on communal preconditions for the appearance of terrorism. The latter approach has almost become mainstream in the field in the last two decades and has tested several communal conditions/dynamics which increase inclinations of communities to implement political violence: economic deprivation—relative or absolute; political and social oppression; collapse of social structure, accompanied by rapid social and economic changes which leave some segments of society behind, also known as the "collective behavior school";[381] the existence of resources, cost-reducing mechanisms or constraints—such as societal support, formal political support, existence of mobilization potential— that impact mobilization of deprived groups or anti-system groups and the abilities of such groups to overcome these constraints or to aggregate resources, known also as "resources mobilization theory"; for example, the emergence of the Skinhead movement could be attributed to the resources provided by veteran organizations such as WAR; and finally the Political Opportunity Structure theory emphasizes the existence of a convenient political-social structure by highlighting that movements and groups' developments and tactics are significantly "…affected by a

---

[379] The following studies confirmed this assertion in the American far right arena. See R. Blazak, "White Boys to Terrorist Men: Target Recruitment of Nazi Skinheads," *American Behavioral Science* 44 (2001), 982–1000; Kathrin M. Blee, *Inside Organized Racism: Women in the Hate Movement* (Berkeley: Univ. Calif. Press, 2002); Hamm.

[380] Pedahzur and Perliger (2006).

[381] For an effective summary of this approach, see Freilich, 31–3.

shifting constellation of factors exogenous to the movement itself."[382] Some of these factors, such as traditions and institutions, are relatively stable and others are more volatile, such as elite alignment, political discourse, and the security situation.[383] Overall, these studies departed from the attempt to explain individual behavior and turned to explaining communal tendencies. While there are many variations and nuances to these communal theories, many suffer from basic methodological-conceptual shortcomings which are also prevalent in the socialization and social networks studies. They cannot detect what characterizes or differentiates those who join violent groups from the rest of the population that is exposed to the same social conditions.

4.4.2 – Theories Explaining Far-Right Activism

Some of the theories focusing on explaining far-right activism are closely related—or are more specific versions—of the above-mentioned political violence theories. This is not a complete surprise, especially since far-right politics in many instances has been characterized by violent practices. Another similarity between the two bodies of literature is related to their evolution; as in the case of the study of far-right activism, scholars initially focused on the personal/psychological traits which characterize those who joined militant far right groups. Adorno's "authoritarian personality" is probably the most renowned study in this context and, like the ones that followed it, argued that those who tend to support far-right ideology have unique mental and personal traits.[384] The mixed empirical support for Adorno's approach, and the dramatic rise in the power of the European far-right during the 1980s and 1990s, led to the emergence of a long list of theories and explanations that departed from the individual-psychological approach: these are summarized in Table 3.

---

[382] David S. Meyer and Suzanne Staggenborg, "Movements, Countermovements, and the Structure of Political Opportunity," *The American Journal of Sociology*, 101(6) (1996), 1628–60.
[383] Ibid.
[384] Theodor W. Adorno, Else Frenkel-Brunswik, Daniel J. Levinson, R. Nevitt Sanford, *Authoritarian Personality* (Oxford, England: Harpers, 1950).

Table 3 – Theories Explaining the Rise/Popularity of Far Right Groups

Theory	Rationale
Single Issue Thesis	The narrow nature of the political message and its relevancy explains success. Main examples which are usually mentioned are the success of far-right groups/parties which have focused on anti-immigration, law and order and unemployment policies. Hence, far-right groups will be successful when one of these issues is at the center of public or political discourse.[385]
The Protest Thesis	Popularity of far-right groups is related to the level of societal discontent with the mainstream established political actors. Thus, support is less ideological but more an expression of temporary frustration with established politics.[386]
Social Breakdown Thesis (Mass Society Theory)	Breakdown of traditional social structure (class, religion) has weakened the sense of social integration, belonging and solidarity: hence, people tend to be attracted to ethnic nationalism. This leads to escalation of group relations and increases anomie which leads to the loss of the foundations for standards of judgment and behavior.[387]
Post Material Thesis	Stresses the importance of traditional values over economic interests. An individual who feels strongly attached to traditional values, when the latter are—according to their perceptions—in decline, are more inclined to join far-right groups. A counter-response to post-material politics which focus on issues such as environment, gender relations, e.g., politics of feminism, etc.[388]

---

[385] For a summary of this approach see Roger Eatwell, *Ten Theories of the Extreme Right*, in ed. Peter H. Merkl and Leonard Weinberg, *Right Wing Extremism in the Twenty First Century* (Portland, Oregon: Frank Cass, 2003), 47–71.

[386] P. Knigge, "The Ecological Correlates of Right-Wing Extremism in Western Europe," *European Journal of Political Research*, 34(2) (1998); Hans Georg Betz, "Conditions Favoring the Success (and Failure) of Radical Right-Wing Populist Parties in Contemporary Democracies," in ed. Y. Meny and Y. Surel, *Democracies and the Populist Challenge* (Basingstoke: Palgrave, 2002).

[387] William Kornhauser, *The Politics of Mass Society* (Glencoe: Free Press, 1959); S. Halebsky, *Mass Society and Political Conflict: Towards a Reconstruction of Theory* (New York: Cambridge University Press, 1976); Eatwell, 52–4.

[388] Paul Ignazi, "The Silent Counter-Revolution: Hypothesis on the Emergence of Extreme- Right Wing Parties in Europe," *European Journal of Political Research*, 26(3) (1992), 3–34.

Status Theories and Economic Interests	Far-right groups emerge in order to maintain narrowing lines of power and privileges. Far-right activism intensifies when specific segments of the population feel that they are losing status and power as a result of economic/normative changes. Some theories directly link economic interests—or a sense of economic insecurity—with support for far-right ideology. [389]
Political Opportunity Structure (POS)	Combination of all or some of the following components can facilitate the emergence and growth of far right groups: weak political structure or turmoil in the political system, external pressure, existence of mobilization resources (when mainstream politics neglect central issues) and legitimization of far-right ideas by mainstream politics.[390]
Growing Heterogeneity of Society	Rapid population growth which results from a high proportion of newcomers facilitates the rise of far-right groups as a result of a decline in community cohesiveness, an increase in social stress and competition over resources. [391]
Mediatization Thesis	The tendency of the media to portray the negative dimensions/aspects of foreign communities, combined with the tendency of far-right groups to nurture highly charismatic leaders explains the success of far-right groups. The narrow and sometimes simplistic nature of far-right ideology is better adapted to the contemporary nature of the political discourse and mass media.[392]
National Tradition Thesis	The success of far right groups depends on their ability to portray themselves as part of the region/country's tradition and heritage. This way they can legitimize their discourse and penetrate the political and social spheres more easily. People are more reluctant to be excluded from political discourse groups which position themselves as part of the community's historical identity.[393]

While some of the ideas presented in Table 3 deserve the designation of theories (POS), as they are based on a clear and developed set of concepts and hypotheses which were

---

[389] S. M. Lipset and E. Rabb, *The Politics of Unreason: Right Wing Extremism in America, 1790–1970* (New York: HarperCollins, 1970).

[390] For theoretical considerations, see H. Kitschelt, "Political opportunity structures and political protest: anti-nuclear movements in four democracies," *British Journal of Political Science*, 16 (1986), 57–85; on its application in the case of the American far right, see Freilich, 34–7.

[391] Lipset and Rabb; J. A. Aho, *Politics of Righteousness: Idaho Christian Patriotism* (Seattle: University of Washington Press, 1990); W. B. Hixson, Jr., *Search for the American Right Wing: An Analysis of the Social Science Record, 1955–1987* (Princeton: Princeton University Press, 1992).

[392] T. A. Van Dijk, *Elite Discourse and Racism* (London, UK: Sage, 1993).

[393] Eatwell, 62–3.

tested empirically, others are simplistic descriptions of the conditions under which far right groups may be more successful. Regardless, they provide basic familiarity with the main direction taken by students of far right groups regarding the factors which explain the rise of their success.

4.4.3 – The American Far-Right in Theoretical Context

It should be clarified from the outset that while some of the theories presented above appear highly applicable for explaining the rise, or trends, of specific movements of the American far right, at this stage the goal remains that of establishing an overarching perspective; the subsequent sections of the study will focus on explaining the trends of the specific streams of the American far right.

The findings presented in the empirical sections earlier indicate a sustained association between the characteristics of the political environment and the level of far right violence. To iterate briefly, times of increasing political competition, i.e., election years, as well as an increase in the power of conservative political forces, are normally accompanied by increased levels of far right violence. Thus, we can carefully argue that this corresponds with some aspects of the POS and Protest theses. Having gained prominence in the study of social movements, POS reflects the tendency to see political activism—particularly in the context of broad social movements—as a result of perceived changes in the political power structure. In the eyes of the movement's members, such activism presents an opportunity to promote significant political change, or in the words of McAdam, "Any event or broad social process that serves to undermine the calculations on which the political establishment is structured occasions a shift in political opportunities."[394] Some students of this approach specifically emphasize the importance of the openness of political institutions to ideas of the movement as a factor that facilitates the rise of the movement. And while most scholars do not tend to see elections as an opportunity, it seems that this is the case in the eyes of far right elements in the United States. The reason for this anomaly may be the relative uniqueness of the American political system.

---

[394] Doug McAdam, *Political Process and the Development of the Black Insurgency, 1930–1970* (Chicago: University of Chicago Press, 1982).

In most parliamentary systems the results of elections are reflected in the restructure of divisions of political power between existing sets of actors and their respective parties; thus in many cases the same actors may serve in various constellations of governmental coalitions. Therefore, results of elections in many instances will lead to marginal changes in major policy issues, especially those related to society's core moral foundations. This is also a result of the fact that coalitions by definition demand compromises, which usually prevent dramatic changes in core policies after elections. There are significant caveats to these generalizations, and sometimes we will witness revolutionary electoral results. Nonetheless, general elections in most parliamentary systems can be described as more incremental in the ways they impact public policies.

The United States in this sense is a different breed. Both the two-party system, which creates the political dynamic and perception of a zero sum game, and the predominant nature of the executive branch, which channels the political game into one major electoral process—the presidential election—may shape a mindset which will perceive every presidential election as an opportunity to promote significant change. This also may explain why the only genuinely non-competitive election in the previous two decades was the only one not accompanied by an increase in the level of far right violence: the 1996 elections were won by a landslide as President Clinton gathered 200 more electoral votes than the Republican candidate, Robert Dole. In such highly non-competitive elections, the electoral processes could not seriously be perceived as an opportunity.

Continuing this line of analysis, the positive correlation between a conservative political environment and high levels of far right violence could indicate that in the eyes of far right elements, periods of conservative political dominance are times of opportunity in which the political system is more accessible and open to pressure from groups on the right side of the political spectrum. Indeed, social movement studies have emphasized the role of perceived success in increasing mobilization and activism.[395] Similarly, studies conducted in the European arena have identified correlations between an increase of support for the far right and legitimization of its ideas by mainstream political actors.[396]

---

[395] Meyer and Staggenborg.
[396] Eatwell, 59.

Finally, this perception is also partially supported by the findings which reflect higher levels of violence following Supreme Court decisions that are more supportive of conservative social values. These decisions may generate the sense of a shift—or a potential shift—in the division of political power among far right activists, and thereby function as a call for seizing the opportunity by further engaging in political activism.

POS theories have attracted significant criticism, mainly because of the subjective and unclear usage of the concept of opportunity, the mixed results of empirical attempts to confirm the theory, and their sometimes limited utility for comparative analysis.[397] On the other hand, the protest thesis is usually easier to use in comparative frameworks, since its main argument is that support and activism in the context of the far right is, in many cases, a result of frustration and distrust of mainstream established political actors. These are feelings that are generally easy to measure. In the American context it has been mentioned that one possible explanation for the higher levels of violence during elections is the inability of far-right groups to penetrate the political system via legitimate means, as well as the marginality of their ideas. Both are even more salient in times of electoral processes: hence, they further encourage radicalization. Simply put, the growing frustration and distrust with the established political parties tend to be more intense during election periods, when it is clear to far right elements that they have no viable platforms for promoting their goals.

However, whereas strong feelings of hostility towards the government and the established parties are to be found to an extent in most far right groups, several factors make application of the protest thesis in the American context problematic. First, as indicated by Eatwell, this thesis assumes that support for the far right is transient and unstructured.[398] However, this is not the case with the American far right, which depicts clear trends over time; moreover, most ethnographical evidence reflects that far right activists are not temporary in the sense assumed in the protest thesis: for extended periods of time many of them remain supporters of specific ideological principles, e.g., anti-abortion, anti-gun legislation. Finally, one should ask why following events which are supposed to lessen levels of frustration—positive electoral results or a more

---

[397] C. A. Rootes, "Political Opportunity Structures: Promise, Problems and Prospects Centre for the Study of Social and Political Movements," Darwin College, University of Kent at Canterbury, http://www.kent.ac.uk/sspssr/staff/academic/rootes/pos.pdf (accessed 4 November 2012).
[398] Eatwell.

supportive composition of the legislative branch—we see an increase in the level of violence rather than a decrease.

The findings related to the geographical characteristics of far right violence are also helpful in assessing the applicability of far right theories to the American case. The national/regional tradition thesis is highly deficient in predicting trends in the American case, as the regions which were the hotbed of the American far right violence for many years have in the last two decades become the periphery of the phenomenon. The fact that this process of transition of violence from the Deep South to other parts of the country has gone hand-in-hand with what appears to be the increasing fragmentation of the movements, may imply that the national/regional tradition thesis is applicable only when there is an existing effective organizational framework. In other words, it is useful only when the tradition is reflected—and on some level preserved by—an existing organizational framework such as an active SMO. The disappearance or weakening of the far right organizational framework in the South may serve to reduce the importance of existing traditions and practices related to far right ideology. This explanation also corresponds with the findings that the great majority of far right violence in the last two decades has been perpetrated by unaffiliated groups and individuals—this issue will be discussed at length in the next section. When collective action is characterized by lack of formality and organizational norms, tradition and heritage, which are usually crucial tools for maintaining the organizational framework, become less important.

In contrast, Lipset and Rab's ideas regarding the association between the level of heterogeneity of the community/region and the level of far right activism are confirmed by the empirical analyses. Nevertheless, understanding the meaning of these findings demands a more careful and nuanced examination. Focusing mainly on newcomers/minorities, Lipset and Rab argue that their arrival in high numbers creates social stress within the affected society and community and weakens communal solidarity, since there are fewer shared norms between members of the community. These are processes that eventually facilitate violence against outsiders. Thus, an important factor in this process is not merely the arrival or presence of minorities/immigrants, but their growing proportion within the particular communities that exhibit far right violence. Indeed, analyses demonstrate correlation between the level of violence and the proportion of certain minority groups. However, here we are facing an interesting contradiction; in the case of the fastest-growing minority group in the United States, the Hispanic population, the findings were not significant. How can this be explained? One not entirely convincing explanation is that we must be more patient: far right groups will eventually adapt operationally and ideologically, so that in the future we will see more attacks in states with higher concentrations of Hispanics. Another explanation cites the identification problem: Hispanic targets/individuals are not as visible as other, more obvious minority groups. Finally, there may be a methodological bias, as it may be assumed that violence against Hispanics usually has less chance of being reported as a hate crime, because many of the victims may be illegal immigrants and because hate crimes are usually associated with hostilities against Jews or African Americans.

The other far right theories appear to be less relevant to the American case; the relatively high ideological diversity of the American far-right—as depicted in the ideological analysis of this study—makes it difficult to see the relevance of the single-issue thesis. As for the mediatization thesis, in the United States the mainstream media is extremely careful about providing access for far right elements. And with regard to theories which focus on changes in social values, social structure, and on the division of political and economic power—Social Breakdown Thesis, Post Material Thesis, Status Theories—these are, in many ways, offspring of the relative deprivation framework, each focusing on different resources and values whose accessibility to the deprived community is in decline. While the current study did not use methodological tools which will allow measurement perceptions of the relevant communities over time in a systematic way, there are some indications which shed doubt on the relevancy of these theories for the American case; their inapplicability is at least evident when trying to develop generalizations which are relevant to the entire American far right. As shown earlier, the association between economic indicators and far right violence is in doubt. Second, how can we explain the decline of violence during eras which experienced dramatic changes in societal values, i.e., the late 1960s and early 1970s? Third, this seems to contradict the association identified earlier between a conservative political environment and an increase in far-right violence. Fourth, the more conservative states are the ones less affected by violence. Finally, while growth in representation of minority or previously deprived groups in political institutions is usually considered to be one of the direct indications of changes in political and economic power divisions, in the case of the American far right it is not easy to find a clear correlation between the two. For example, Figure 11 illustrates that the breakthrough in terms of representation of minority groups in the Congress for African Americans and Hispanics occurred in the early 1990s; however, these periods were characterized by relatively low levels of violence. More specifically, the period after the 1992 elections—which saw the most dramatic increase in the number of minority members in Congress, from 73 to 97, or from 32 to 55 excluding Jewish members of Congress—was followed by a significant decrease in the level of violence.

Figure 11 –Members of Congress Belonging to Minority Groups by Year

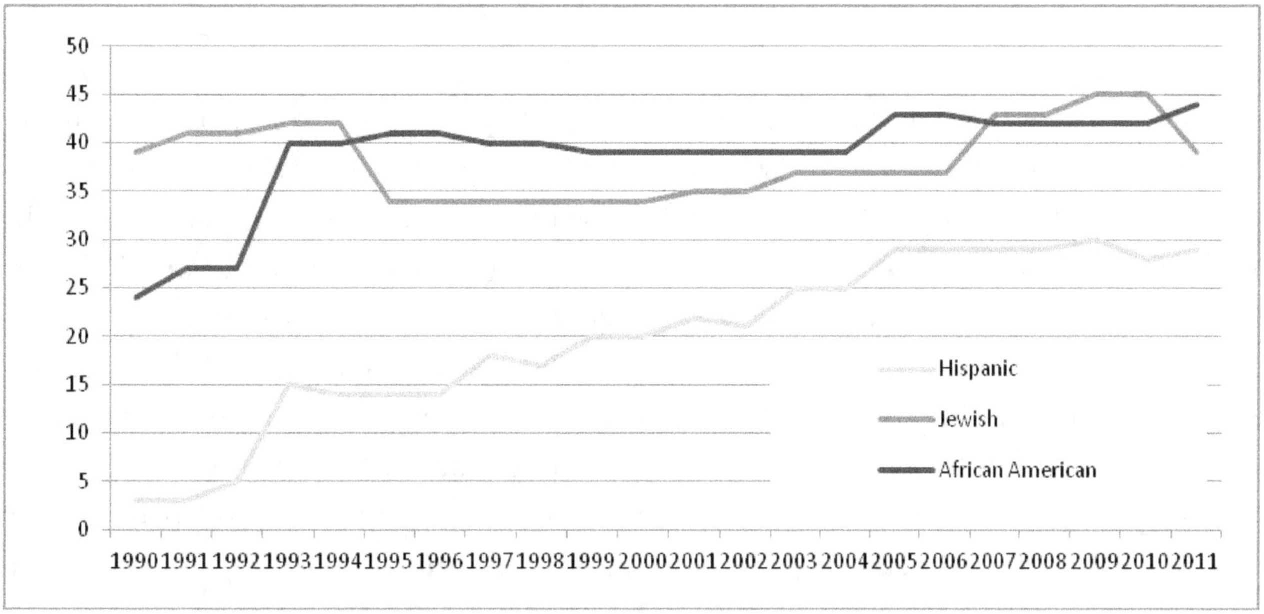

How do these findings hold when examining the distinct components of the American far-right? The following section will provide insights regarding specific movements/groups which will help answer this key question.

5. Empirical Picture: The Perpetrators and Trends among Specific Movements

While so far this study has focused on macro-level trends, the current chapter will adopt a higher resolution. Following a basic introduction to the nature of the perpetrators, subsequent sections will try to provide an improved understanding of the operational and demographic characteristics of the different movements comprising the American far-right. A comparative analysis which will focus mainly on the level of threat posed by the various groups will conclude the chapter.

5.1 - The Perpetrators

While the desire to devise a consensual sociological profile of terrorists is still a major goal for many students of terrorism, a growing number of scholars acknowledge that this task may be out of reach; this is less because of data limitations—in recent years the number of available datasets detailing terrorists' demographic characteristics has been increasing rapidly—and more because a growing amount of empirical evidence implies that such a universal profile may not exist.[399] These scholars argue that the profile is both dependent on the role, status and seniority of the member of the group, and on the cultural and political context in which the group operates. Moreover, they criticize the tendency to ignore the impact of the time variable and, in particular, the inclination to ignore the fact that the demographics of group members may change over time and that individuals' biographies also change and evolve.[400]

Whereas the current study does not aim to provide a sociological profile of perpetrators of far-right violence, it attempts to address two related issues which for many years were perceived as almost paradigmatic in the field of terrorism studies. The first is the assertion that political violence in general and terrorism specifically constitute collective action. Ariel Merari, to illustrate, has argued that 95 percent of all suicide terrorist attacks are perpetrated by groups.[401] Historically this perception has been echoed in the writings of most scholars of terrorism, as many have analyzed terrorism using various organizational and social theories. It is therefore interesting to note that in the context of

---

[399] See e.g., Horgan; Victoroff.

[400] Ibid.

[401] Ariel Merari, *Driven to Death: Psychological and Social Aspects of Suicide Terrorism* (Oxford: Oxford University Press, 2010).

the violent American far right some of the more notable perpetrators have been viewed as what is referred to as lone wolves: autonomous individuals not reliant upon far-right organizations. Sometimes this designation has been justified, as in the case of Eric R. Rudolph, while at other times it has been the result of a popular misconception, as in the case of Timothy McVeigh. But are such infamous cases any indication of a recognizable trend, or they should be regarded as outliers?

The percentages cited in Figure 12—which classifies far right attacks based on the number of perpetrators—reflect a surprising reality. The great majority of attacks were perpetrated by a single individual or two perpetrators at most. Less than one third of the attacks were carried out by what we can call a group, i.e., three or more perpetrators. How can this discrepancy between the American far-right and other types of terrorism be explained?

Figure 12 – Far Right Attacks by Number of Perpetrators

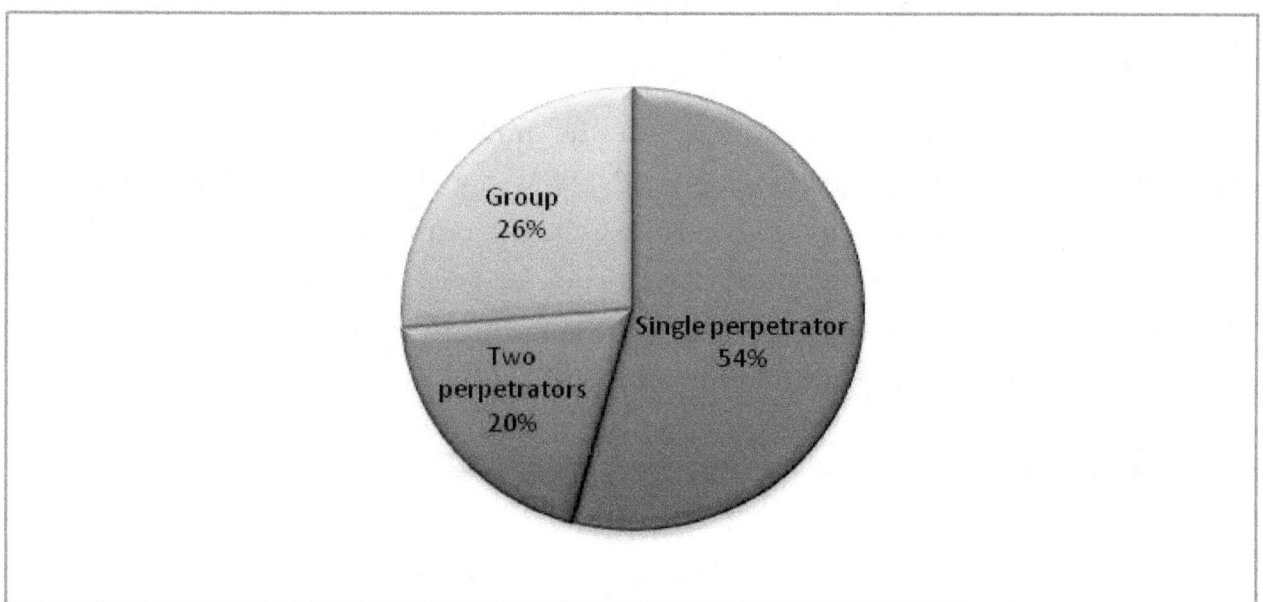

First, words of caution are necessary. The perpetrators of 40% of the attacks in the dataset were never caught or identified; it is therefore impossible to know exactly how many perpetrators were involved. While this is not surprising, considering the nature of the phenomenon; and despite the fact that the sample size of the attacks with identified perpetrators is extremely large (2,649 attacks) in comparison to similar datasets, care is still demanded regarding any possible conclusions. Second, the findings may reflect a further, more extreme implementation of the leaderless resistance doctrine, which has been promoted by various leaders of the American far right during the last two decades. Thus, it seems that their words have not fallen on deaf ears. The findings may also indicate an interesting operational path which, on the one hand, ensures the survival of the organization, and on the other hand, allows it to engage indirectly in violent activities. In other words, while the organization as a whole cannot afford to be directly involved in sponsoring and perpetrating a violent campaign, since the legal and organizational implications may be costly, especially in the American/Western context of highly qualified and efficient law enforcement, it encourages individual members to engage in violent activities which are not directly part of the organizational operational framework. This strategy may not work in cases of extreme manifestations of violence — e.g., the loose and previous affiliation of McVeigh with the Michigan Militia, which eventually led to a harsh response against the militia movement after the attack in Oklahoma — but may be effective in cases of minor attacks. Moreover, considering that one of the most efficient countermeasures against far right groups during the 1980s and the 1990s was civilian law suits, the importance in distancing a given group from a direct link to attacks is further evident.

Finally, the findings also help to explain the limited level of sophistication and development of the American far right. ANOVA model[402] has found that there are significant gaps in terms of the number of casualties produced by attacks initiated by 1–2 members and attacks which are the production of groups (F=3.895*; see also Figure 13). Thus, notwithstanding the advantages of the leaderless resistance doctrine, it seems to incur costs in terms of the productivity of the violence.

Figure 13 – Average Number of Casualties by Number of Perpetrators

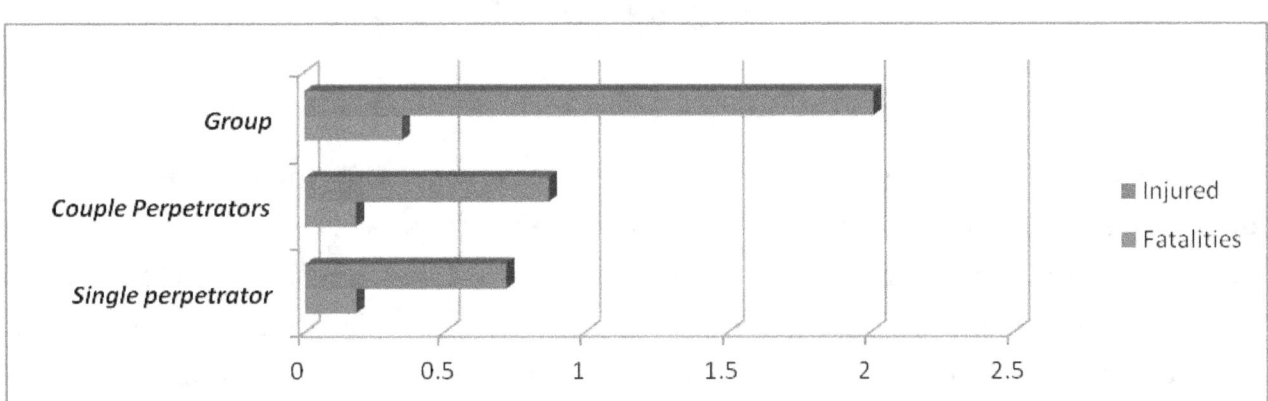

---

[402] ANOVA (Analysis of Variance) is a collection of statistical models which helps to test whether the gaps in the means of several groups are statistically significant.

A second perception which enjoys consensus within the academic community is related to the terrorists' young age. This is usually explained by the concept of biographical availability; simply put, people with limited commitments—individuals who are single, with no permanent jobs or career path, and with limited social ties—are more prone to risky activities such as terrorism than people with limited biographical availability.[403] And since biographical availability usually becomes increasingly limited as the individual matures, the dominant perception is that young people are far more likely to be inclined to join violent groups. Is this perception also true in the case of the American far right?

In order to answer this question, data regarding the age of 2,221 perpetrators of attacks documented in the far-right attack dataset were analyzed. As expected, the average age of the perpetrators was relatively low (25.61). A closer look however, reveals a more interesting picture (see Figure 14). As expected, most perpetrators were in their 20s (39.6%); nevertheless, a high number of attacks—close to half—were conducted by the very young (below 20: 35%) or by relatively mature individuals (above 40: 12.3%). This exemplifies the diversity of actors involved in far right violence, as well as providing probable further confirmation of the perception presented above regarding the limited current institutionalization of far right violence. In an environment in which violence is a product of independent individuals and small networks, the conventional gatekeepers who limit the involvement of members who are too young or too old in operations are less effective.

---

[403] Gregory Wiltfang and Doug McAdam, "Distinguishing Cost and Risk in Sanctuary Activism," *Social Forces* 69 (1991), 987–1010

Figure 14 – Perpetrators of Far Right Violence by Age

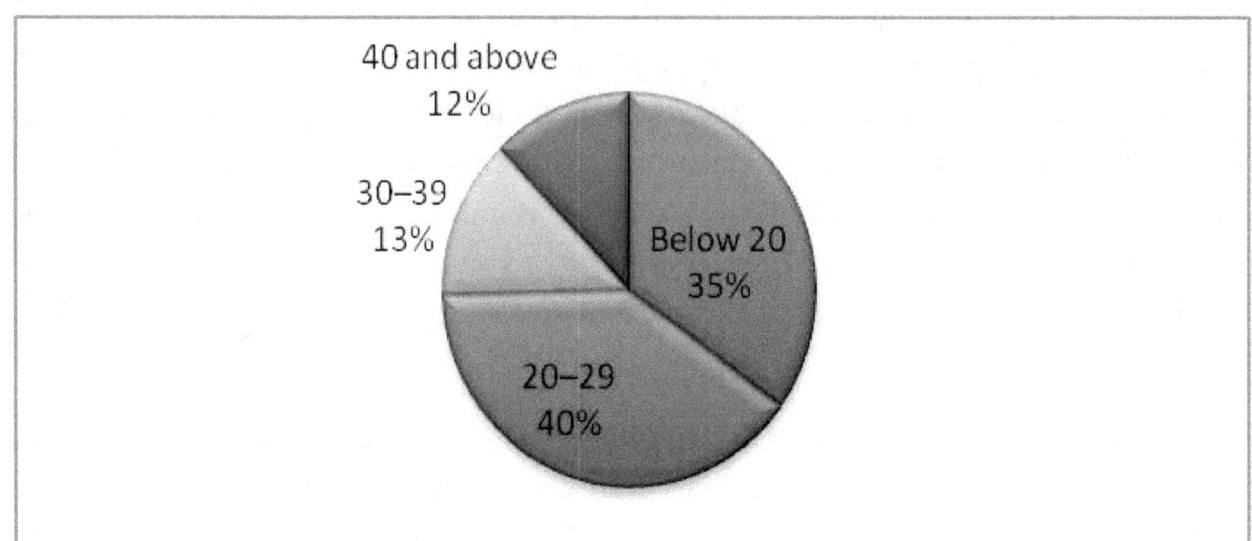

5.2 – The Racist/White Supremacy Movement

5.2.1 – Analyzing KKK (and affiliates') Violence

The dataset documents 593 attacks perpetrated by groups which are part of the racist movement. Almost a third of these attacks (264) were perpetrated by the KKK and close affiliates.

As mentioned in the first part of this study, since the 1980s the KKK has suffered a continuous decline in terms of affiliated members, influence and importance. This was partly a result of the financial drain from civilian law suits against chapters of the organization.[404] It is partially due to the rise of more attractive alternatives.[405] Also, internal clashes and disagreements led many prominent leaders to desert the movement and join other far right groups. Moreover, while a number of Klans had aspired to develop into nationwide organizations and were able to establish branches in several states—such as the *United Klans of America, Knights of the Ku Klux Klan, Federation of*

---

[404] For example, in 1987 the *United Klans of America* ended its operation in the wake of an Alabama jury award of $7 million against the organization once its members were found guilty of lynching a young African American man. In another case in 1998 a jury in South Carolina ordered two Ku Klux Klan chapters (*Christian Knights of the Ku Klux Klan* and *Invisible Empire, Inc.*) to pay $37.8 million to the Macedonia Baptist Church after members of the groups were found to be involved in a series of arson attacks against the church.

[405] The growth of the militia movement and the Christian Identity groups were mainly responsible for the difficulties of the KKK mobilization efforts: Southern Poverty Law Center Klanwatch Staff, 45, 48–51.

Klans: Knights of the Ku Klux Klan and the *Church of the National Knights of the Ku Klux Klan*—they all met with limited success in reviving the movement. Thus, the KKK today should be understood more as a collection of independent small groups which shares similar terminology, ideological tendencies and historical references, but lacks meaningful cooperation and coordination.

In order to overcome the above mentioned recruitment challenges, some of the relatively new Klans have chosen to adopt ideological components and recruitment mechanisms that were traditionally used by other far-right groups, and to address contemporary issues in their propaganda. For instance, *The Imperial Klans of America*—founded in 1996 by Ron Edwards and one of the more prominent KKK groups in the late 1990s and early 2000s—adopted ideological elements from the Christian Identity movement, including its own version of the story of Genesis and conspiracy theories about Jewish control of global media and local governments. They organized an Annual racist Nordic-Fest music festival, and in the second half of the first decade of the 2000s began to emphasize the necessity to fight illegal immigration in its published propaganda.[406] Thus, IKA employed the classic recruitment mechanism of the Skinheads movement music festival, borrowed fundamentalist ideas from the Christian Identity movement, and exploited a contemporary controversial political issue to maintain its relevancy and expand its ranks. Notwithstanding this, and despite short-term success, the IKA suffered the same fate as other KKK groups when in 2008 it lost a $2.5 million civil suit following a group member's violent attack against an individual in Kentucky who he suspected was Latino. Consequently, while still active the group lost most of its members and assets.[407]

---

[406] See IKA profile, Southern Poverty Law Centre, "Intelligence Files: Imperial Klans of America— Ron Edwards," http://www.splcenter.org/get-informed/intelligence-files/groups/imperial-klans-of-america (accessed 4 November 2012).
[407] Ibid.

Figure 15 – Number of Attacks by KKK and Affiliates by Year

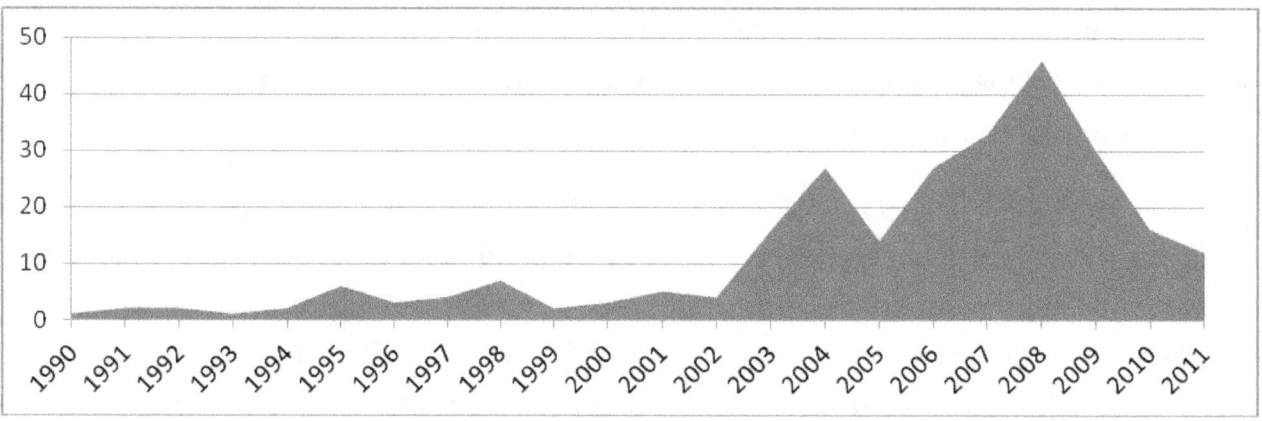

To summarize, the KKK currently includes between 5,000 and 10,000 members who are spread across 150 independent chapters located mostly in the South (mainly in the states of Alabama, Arkansas, Florida, Georgia, Indiana, Mississippi, North Carolina, Tennessee and Texas). However, can we identify more empirical and systematic signs of the KKK's decline and of its concentration in the South? The answer is not definitive. As can be observed in Figure 15, most of the KKK attacks occurred in the last decade, corresponding with the general trend of American far right violence; while the numbers are low, we can definitely say that in the last decade there has been an increase in the number of attacks initiated by individuals and groups affiliated with the KKK. Nonetheless, precisely because this is compatible with the general far right trend, it is problematic to see it as a clear indication of the group's impact within the far right arena, and thus of its decline.

In order to assess this issue there is a need to consider the proportion of KKK attacks as a component of overall acts of far right violence. Figure 16, which reflects this, describes a more complicated reality. To begin with, over the years KKK violence has consistently constituted a small part of overall far right violence: a dramatic change from the situation in the 1950s and the 1960s, when the organization held a monopoly on the American far right violent struggle. Moreover, instead of a continuous decline of the KKK's role within the far right, we can observe flashes of significant activism in some years during the 1990s and a substantial presence between 2003 and 2008. Lastly, it is important to wait for the availability of more data points before concluding whether the decline in the proportion of KKK violence, which began in 2008, is temporary or is an indication of further accelerated decline.

Figure 16 – Proportion of KKK Attacks of Overall Far Right Violence by Year

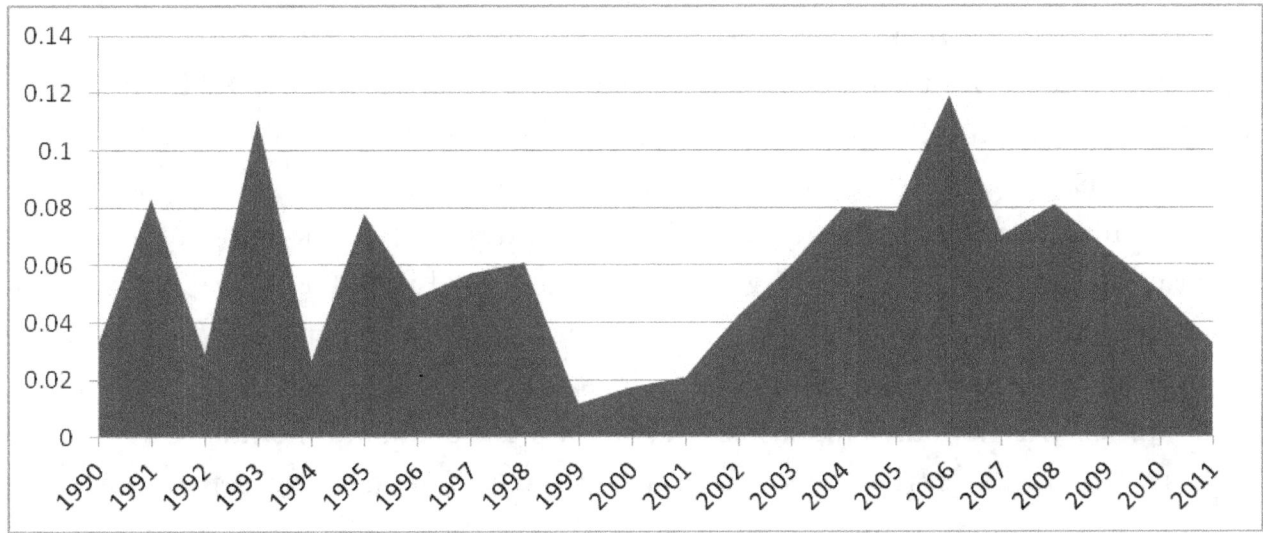

As mentioned earlier in this study, KKK violence is no longer concentrated in the Deep South. Nonetheless, most indications are that the majority of active KKK branches operate in this region; according to SPLC documentation, 107 out of the existing 152 branches are located in southern states. This may be another indication of the declining relevance of the movement, or simply a reflection of the fact that while other movements of the American far right moved out of the South, for historical and cultural reasons the KKK is still mostly important to people in these regions. The numbers tell us that the answer is somewhere in between. While the majority of KKK attacks did not take place in the South (119 out of 264: 45%—this includes Florida but excludes Maryland), a significant proportion of the violence is still concentrated in this region. Moreover, closer scrutiny reveals that most of the attacks occur in the South or in one of the three following states: Maryland, Pennsylvania and California; all of the other states experienced a one-digit number of attacks in the previous 22 years, except for New York, with 10 attacks. To conclude, the operational base of the KKK is also beginning to shift to other regions of the country. However, it is doing so at a much slower rate than that of other groups of the American far right.[408]

---

[408] Another possibility is that the overall transition of far right violence from the south to other regions is a reflection of the decline of the KKK. The findings in graphs 15 and 16 tend to mitigate against this explanation.

One of the goals of this study was to garner more information concerning the relative threat posed by the various American far right groups. Hence, in this and the following sections, the unique operational characteristic of each one of the groups will be discussed. In the summary section of this chapter, a comparison between the groups will be presented in order to rank them in accordance with the level of threat that they represent. In line with the movement's ideology, the great majority of KKK attacks are directed against minority groups or related targets (90.2%). In this context the three most popular targets are people (75%: in many cases, the individual's property), religious institutions (7.6%) and educational facilities (4.5%) belonging to a specific minority group. Other types of targets usually associated with far right violence, such as law enforcement representatives, government officials, individuals with alternative sexual orientation and abortion-related facilities, make up only a marginal proportion of KKK attacks. This not only emphasizes the one-dimensional nature of the KKK but also suggests that in the case of the American far right, ideological tendencies have the potential to shape the nature of group violence. Hence, the ideological typology that has been presented in the first part of this study also has an operational manifestation.

KKK perpetrators have focused on relatively vulnerable targets, in contrast to groups which attack law enforcement, financial institutions, etc. Despite this, the results of the violence do not compare with the halcyon days of mass lynching during the mid-1950s and 1960s: in the last 22 years the organization has been responsible for the deaths of 20 individuals and the injuries of another 100, averaging 0.39 injured and 0.07 fatalities per attack. When combining this with the findings that more than two thirds of the attacks were directed against property and just three percent could be described as mass-casualty attacks, it is clear that the contemporary KKK has limited involvement in sophisticated violence. Indeed, even a cursory look at the list of attacks will reveal that many of them have been spontaneous acts of violence against passersby from minority groups, minor vandalism against religious and educational facilities, and similar unsophisticated acts.

To conclude, it is difficult to see any tendency on the part of the current branches of the KKK to engage in systematic campaigns of violence as we have seen in the past, and even when some of their members are involved in violence it is usually opportunity based or spontaneous, and lacks sophistication.

5.2.2 – Analyzing Neo-Nazi and Skinhead Violence

The neo-Nazi and Skinhead groups comprise the younger components of the racist/white Supremacy movement. Neo-Nazis garnered momentum in the late 1950s and Skinheads in the late 1980s. Besides youth, the similarities between these streams are also reflected in the adoption by both groups of European ideologies emphasizing Nazi concepts and cultural practices, and which have gone through processes of fragmentation. In the case of the neo-Nazi groups this happened following the decline of the ANP in the late 1960s, and in the case of the Skinheads, following the decline of the Hammerskins Nation in the mid-1990s. Thus, in many ways their overall organizational structure resembles that of the KKK. In both cases we are dealing with ideological frameworks without clear national leadership comprised of numerous independent local branches.

This is not to say that we cannot identify prominent groups that have dominated the ideological streams. There is little doubt among students of the American far-right as to the importance of the *National Alliance* (NA) for the growth and consolidation of the *Neo Nazi* stream during the 1980s, 1990s and 2000s. The NA was founded in 1970 by William Pierce, author of *Turner Diaries* and probably the most important ideologue among American neo-Nazis. While during most of the 1970s the group was unable to expand and remained a small cultish organization serving Pierce, this changed as *Turner Diaries* began to gain popularity during the 1980s and 1990s. Pierce was able to exploit the growing popularity of his novel to construct an effective business model based on members' fees, income from the distribution and sales of NA propaganda, as well as from the popular white power music label *Resistance Records*, purchased from former Skinheads by Pierce in 1999. Thus, in the early 2000s the 1,400 paying members of the organization enjoyed more than a million-dollar annual income, which allowed it to expand its influence throughout the country, and forge collaborations with similar organizations across the Atlantic, eventually creating chapters in several European countries.[409]

---

[409] ADL, "Extremism in America: National Alliance," *Anti-Defamation League,* http://www.adl.org/learn/ext_us/n_alliance.asp (accessed 4 November 2012).

However, the sudden death of Pierce in 2002 initiated a number of factors that reversed the ascendant course of the group and caused its swift decline in size and influence: internal rivalries; growing resentment towards Pierce's successors from the neo-Nazi and Skinhead community—Erice Gliebe, who replaced Pierce as the NA leader and his second in command, Shaun Walker, showed limited competence in handling NA relations with other neo-Nazi groups; and the declining popularity of the NA music label and publications, which was a byproduct of growing consumer resentment towards the organization. Today most estimates are that the organization includes less than 100 paying members.[410]

The vacuum left by the decline of NA was filled mainly by the *National Socialist Movement* (NSM), which in many ways became the heir of the ANP. This was not merely because of its tendency to engage mainly in public and provocative non-violent initiatives that attracted significant media coverage, following the ANP tradition perfected by Gorge Rockwell and focusing on theatrical parades and demonstrations in sensitive locations and dates; it was also because of its propensity to imitate the practices and protocols of the ANP meticulously, including requiring members to wear full Nazi attire during its events, and the extensive use of Nazi terminology.[411] Several factors facilitated the expansion of the NSM during this period including: a focus on public protests—which limited risk to its members; a willingness to acknowledge dual membership, whereby members of other organizations were permitted to join the group without the need to revoke previous associations; substantial media coverage; and the extremely young age of its leadership - which led to collaboration with Skinhead groups, and helped in attracting young members.[412] Currently the organization includes more than 55 branches in 39 states. In contrast to the KKK, the South is not where most of them or other neo-Nazi groups are concentrated: only 38.5% of the 171 neo-Nazi groups and branches currently active in the United States are located in the historic hub of the American far right.

---

[410] Ibid.

[411] See *National Socialist Movement,* http://www.nsm88.org/ (accessed 4 November 2012).

[412] Although the group was originally established after the murder of Rockwell by former ANP members under the name *Socialist American Workers Freedom Movement,* its modern version was constituted in 1994 under its current name by Jeff Schoep, who was 21 years old at the time. See - ADL, "Extremism in America: National Socialist Movement," *Anti-Defamation League.* http://www.adl.org/Learn/Ext_US/nsm/default.asp?LEARN_Cat=Extremism&LEARN_SubCat=Extremis m_in_America&xpicked=3&item=nsm (accessed 4 November 2012).

The Skinheads also witnessed the rise of distinct dominant groups. The rise and decline of the *Hammerskins Nation*—the most successful organizational manifestation of the American Skinhead scene—has already been discussed in the first part of this study. Several other organizational frameworks have achieved success within the Skinhead scene in the last decade, filling the vacuum left by the HSN: some reports argue that today HSN does not include more than several hundred members. The most notable organizational frameworks among the non-Hammerskin federation are probably *Volksfront* and *The Vinlanders*, also known as *Vinlander Social Club* (VSC).

Established formally in 2003 by Eric "The Butcher" Fairburn and Brian James in an attempt to instill order into the anti-HSN/*Outlaw-Hammerskins* scene, VSC can be described as a loose organizational network that bonds various Skinhead groups, mainly from the Western Northeast, the Midwest (*Pennsylvania's Keystone State Skinheads, Hoosier State Skinheads, Ohio State Skinheads, New Jersey Skinheads, Arizona's Canyon State Skinheads*) and the South. It is coordinated by an annual meeting of the leaders of the various groups, termed *Council 28*.[413] VSC practiced extreme violence against its competition within the Skinheads counterculture: mainly the *Hammerskin Nation*. Ideologically, it emphasized a combination of neo-Nazi/racist ideas and Nordic, Odinist pagan rituals.[414] There are some indications of moderation in the organization since 2007, following the arrest of a number of its major leaders and the announcement of a truce with HSN, but considering its loose structure and boundaries, as well as its lack of hierarchy, this trend may not persist. Estimates are that currently the organization includes several hundred members spread throughout several dozen independent teams across the country.

Volksfront is less influential in comparison to HSN and VSC. It was officially formed in 1994 by Randal Lee Krager in Portland, Oregon, and in most years has expanded quickly, establishing an impressive line of publications including the *Folk Tribune*, the official e-zine of the movement. It has affiliated branches in other cities in the United States, especially on the West coast, and in other English speaking countries including Canada, UK and Australia, and engages in various mass social activities such as conferences, music festivals and internet radio. It also purchases land with the long-

---

[413] The first meeting was conducted in 2005: the second in 2006 ended with what is known today as the "Memorial Day Beatdown" for the violence which erupted during the meeting between several rival groups: see also Southern Poverty Law Center Intelligence Project.
[414] Odinism is a Germanic Neo-Pagan religion.

term aspiration to establish an all-white territory. In contrast to VSC, it seems that *Volksfront's* relations with other Skinhead groups including with the HSN have been less contentious and more elitist in terms of its members. While VSC was highly inclusive, in particular to the more violent elements of the Skinhead counterculture, the *Volksfront* was far stricter in filtering members who did not comply with the organizational honor code: in principle, sex offenders, those lacking high school diplomas and substance abusers were not permitted to join *Volksfront*. Notwithstanding these differences, *Volksfront* followed VSC steps, and several times during the last few years it has renounced the use of violent practices. These statements have usually met with skepticism by most experts of the American far right. The following empirical analysis, among other things, may help to determine whether this skepticism is well-placed.

According to the far right attacks dataset, 329 attacks have been conducted by Skinheads and neo-Nazi groups in the last 22 years. Of these, 205 attacks were perpetrated by Skinheads, and 124 by neo-Nazis. At least in the case of Skinheads it appears that there is compatibility between the public profile and reputation of groups and their involvement in violence: VSC and affiliates (18 attacks), HSN (13) and *Volksfront* (9 attacks) are also prominent in the stream in terms of the number of attacks in which they were involved. Nonetheless, their proportion of the overall attacks is not as significant as we would expect. Moreover, other Skinheads groups which usually receive less attention appear to be no less violent. These include groups such as *Public Enemy No. 1* (PENI) and *Connecticut White Wolves*. To conclude, from an organizational perspective, the current Skinhead violent landscape appears extremely fragmented.

From a geographical perspective, the most prominent trend in Skinhead violence is its concentration in the Western part of the country: 106 attacks (51.7% of all documented Skinhead attacks) occurred in the 3 states of California, Oregon and Arizona. Moreover, except for Connecticut (10 attacks, mostly by the *Connecticut White Wolves*), Florida (9 attacks), Pennsylvania (8 attacks), Nevada (8 attacks) and Texas (7 attacks) no other state suffered more than 5 attacks. Thus, we may carefully claim that the Skinhead violence is a regional rather than a national phenomenon.

The examination of the level of violence of the Skinhead counterculture over time also reveals surprising trends. Whereas during the years 2008–2010 the level of far-right violence was at its highest volume at least since 1990, Skinhead violence declined in those years in comparison to previous years: 55 attacks between 2005 and 2007 in comparison to 21 during 2008–2010. To illustrate, in 2008, which was the most violent year in terms of far right violence, the Skinheads perpetrated their lowest number of attacks per year since 1998. This may imply that there is a need to take seriously the alleged transformation that was declared by groups such as VSC and *Volksfront*, which in the late 2000s announced their transformation into a fraternity/social movement and distanced themselves from violent practices. The VSC announced on its official website that "we left what we considered to be the organized White Nationalist movement in 2007 and have since then concentrated on promoting a combination of more moderate political pursuits as well as our own unique Nordic-based Warrior lifestyle and culture..."[415] *Volksfront's* website, which in 2001 announced its intention to abandon violence, describes itself today in similar terms, using the designation of "Secular Fraternal Organization" which

> ...does not tolerate illegal activity as a group, nor will we accept the lies and slander leveled at our brotherhood by police, the cowards of media, hysteric Zionist fund-raising groups and anarcho-communist terrorist sympathizers. It is a fact that *Volksfront* members are far less likely per capita to commit any crime than members of the United States Congress or radical Leftist organizations.[416]

The decline of Skinhead violence may be a positive development not just for the obvious law and order-related reasons, but also because numbers demonstrate that their attacks tend to be more lethal and sophisticated in comparison to the violence of their older counterparts in the racialist movement, i.e., the KKK. They generate 0.73 injured and 0.24 fatalities per attack, which is 150% more lethal than the KKK. When looking at their target selection, and especially at their tactics, it is easy to understand why. The Skinheads almost never engaged in vandalism (4%) and the great majority of their attacks have been aimed against specific individuals/groups of foreign origin (over 70%: mostly minorities). This is far different from what we found in the case of the KKK, in which more than two thirds of the attacks were against property.

---

[415] See *Vinlanders Social Club*, http://vinlanders.com/ (accessed 4 November 2012).
[416] This was taken originally from the *Volksfront* website. However, in August 2012 the organization announced its complete dissolution, thus the organization's website, blog and face book page were eliminated. It is unclear if the organization will be replaced with other organizational frameworks, less venerable from a legal perspective; apparently the decision was a result of what the *Volksfront* leadership termed "harassment" and investigations by the U.S. government.

Finally, the social dimension of the violence also seems to distinguish between the KKK and Skinhead violence, although in this case the gaps are less substantial. While just 28% of KKK attacks were perpetrated by groups, 39% of Skinhead attacks were perpetrated by groups, thus confirming the perception that Skinhead teams enjoyed higher levels of social density than any other far right group. This assumption is also reinforced to an extent by the relatively high level of in-group violence within the movement (9% of attacks), which is the highest among all components of the American far right.

The same operational trends which were observed and described in the case of Skinheads were also manifested in the case of the neo-Nazi groups' violence. This further confirms the close relations between the two streams, as well as the relations between ideological tendencies and operational characteristics. Simply put, since both countercultures share similar norms and practices, this is translated into similar violent trends. In summary of the similarities, neo-Nazi violence is concentrated on the West Coast: 43.5% of the incidents occurred in California and almost half if we include Arizona. It appears to be in decline since 2008: 34 incidents occurred between 2006 and 2008, in comparison with 16 in the three following years. It also focuses mainly on attacks against individuals and groups of people from foreign origin (65.3% of attacks) or alternative sexual orientation (7.4%). Despite the fact that the proportion of attacks against property (16.9%) is higher than what we find in the case of the Skinheads, it is still much lower than in the KKK. That explains why neo-Nazi violence is significantly more lethal than that of the KKK (1.65 injured and 0.35 fatalities per attack). Finally, two specific groups appear to be more active than the others in the neo-Nazi realm. The first is the *National Alliance* (10.5% of attacks), a finding which corresponds with its dominance within the movement in the last 30 years; the second group is the *Nazi Low Riders* (29%), a criminal network based mainly in California. Its high level of violence partially explains the West Coast predominance of the neo-Nazi violent scene.

5.2.3 – Analyzing Militia Violence

The first part of this study analyzed the relatively short history of the modern militia movement, ending with the assertion that the mid-1990s repetition of political, social and economic developments of the last few years—recession; a democratic administration; expansion of federal involvement in local policies; and growing prominence of immigration and environmental issues—may provide a convenient foundation for the revival of the movement. Indeed, in 2009 the SPLC published a report that argued that the Militias had returned, designating the phenomenon as the "Second Wave." And while the report is careful not to argue that the current level of Militia activities and violence is similar to that of the mid-1990s, and also does not provide any concrete numbers, it does provide a collection of testimonies by local and federal law enforcement agents who argue that there is a definite increase in the number of active militia groups and in their size.[417] In subsequent publications, the SPLC confirm these assessments with numerical data, indicating that while in 2008 less than 50 militia groups were active in the United States, in 2012 the number had risen by over 600% to more than 330, in addition to another almost 1000 associations which promote anti-taxation and anti-federal ideology.

Another development that may be responsible for the growing concerns and awareness of a revival of the militia movement is the growing popularity of the *Sovereign Citizens* (SC). Simply put, the SC opposes formal governmental regulation of their "rights" which they define in highly expansive terms. For example, SC members refuse to apply for a driver's license and car registration— because they believe the Federal government should not regulate their right to drive. SC members also refuse to pay income tax because they view this as an infringement on their right to work for a living. One of the movement's prominent ideologues, Richard McDonald, established State Citizen Service Centers around the country and provides one of the more popular rationales for these practices:

> By metaphysical refinement, in examining our form of government, it might be correctly said that there is no such thing as a citizen of the United States. But constant usage—arising from convenience, and perhaps necessity, and dating from the formation of the Confederacy—has given substantial existence to the idea which the term conveys. A citizen of any one of the States of the Union, is held to be, and called a citizen of the United States, although technically and abstractly there is no such thing. To conceive a citizen of the United States who is not a citizen of some one of the states, is totally foreign to the idea, and inconsistent with the proper construction and common understanding of the expression as used in the constitution, which must be deduced from its various other provisions...therefore, prior to the alleged ratification of the 14th Amendment, there was no legal definition of a

---

[417] Southern Poverty Law Center, *Second Wave: Return of the Militias*, August (2009).

"citizen of the United States", as everyone had primary citizenship in one of the several states. The Constitution referred to the sovereign state citizen, and no one else…. In other words, you do not have to be a citizen of the United States in order to be a state citizen. This was held to be true by the Maryland Supreme Court in 1966 wherein the state:

Both before and after the Fourteenth Amendment to the federal Constitution, it has not been necessary for a person to be a citizen of the United States in order to be a citizen of his state (*Crosse v. Bd. of Supervisors of Elections*, 221 A.2d. 431 (1966)).

…The federal government was never given any authority to encroach upon the private affairs of the citizens in the several states of the union, unless they were involved in import or export activity, neither were they given authority to reach a citizen of Germany living in Germany. In fact, the states could refuse to enforce any act of congress that they felt was outside the intent of the granting of limited powers to the federal government. This is called interposition or nullification. Several state supreme courts have in the past refused to uphold federal laws within their states.[418]

Several violent incidents involving SC members, including the killing of two West Memphis, Arkansas police officers during a traffic stop in May 2010, indicated that some members of the group were willing to use violence in support of their ideology. But does a recognizable trend within the anti-federalist movement exist? The subsequent empirical examination of the movement's violence may provide an answer.

Our dataset documented 87 cases of violent attacks that were initiated by militias or other anti-federal associations between 1990 and 2011. As expected, almost half of the attacks were perpetrated during the movement's popular period, the second half of the 1990s (48.2%). Since then we have witnessed limited violent activities by the militias, except for a sharp rise during 2010 of 13 attacks. Nonetheless, in 2011 the number returns to the level observed in previous years (between 1–4 attacks per year; 2 attacks in 2011). Thus, while there may be a rise in the number of active militia groups, except for 2010 we still do not see this systematically manifested in the level of violence. As for the geographical dispersion of the attacks, California again is highly prominent (18.4%) alongside Texas (10.3%). The rest of the attacks are distributed more or less equally

---

[418] Richard McDonald, "*Citizen or* citizen?" http://freedom-school.com/citizenship/citizen-or-citizen.html (accessed 4 November 2012).

among 28 other states. The areas that are excluded are parts of the northeast: no attacks were reported in New York, New Jersey, Connecticut, Delaware, Maine, Vermont, Rhode Island, and there was only one attack each in Massachusetts and New Hampshire; the northern Midwest: there were no attacks in Illinois, Iowa, North and South Dakota; and some Southern states: Kentucky, Louisiana, Mississippi and Missouri. Thus, it is difficult to find a geographic rationale for the violence.

When analyzing the violence of the groups comprising the racist movement, we find a consistent association between ideological characteristics and operational tendencies. The same trend is observable when looking into the target selection of the militias, as two-thirds of the attacks were directed against the government and its proxies/law enforcement (66.2%); while attacks against minorities (8.4%) and infrastructure (6%, which could also be seen as an attacks against the government) comprised most of the rest. Thus, despite growing indications that the militias are influenced by the racist and xenophobic rhetoric of neighboring organizations in the far right universe, this is not reflected in the militias' violence, a point that is also confirmed by analysis which demonstrates that attacks against minorities have not risen in recent years.

The emphasis of militias on attacks against physical targets associated with the collective's unifying ethos and existing dominant values and practices may provide another explanation for the growing concerns regarding their activity, despite their relatively limited violence. Inflicting damage on symbolic targets enhances the sense of vulnerability of the existing political order but, more importantly, it is perceived by policymakers as a threat to their ability to maintain government dominance in shaping the political and social discourse. As a side note, attacks against symbolic targets have the potential to increase hostility toward terrorists, as well as expanding the social and emotional distance between terrorists and the collective and, as a result, legitimizing or encouraging a harsher response. [419]

Another element that may be related to the concerns regarding Militia activities is the perception that they are typically engaged in high-casualty attacks. Before testing this

---

[419] Arie Perliger, "How Democracies Respond to Terrorism: Regime Characteristics, Symbolic Power and Counterterrorism," *Security Studies* 21, no. 3 (2012), 490-528; Schmid and Jongman, 83; Bruce Hoffman, "Terrorist Targeting: Tactics, Trends, and Potentialities," *Terrorism and Political Violence* 5, no. 2 (1993), 12–29; C. J. M. Drake, "The Role of Ideology in Terrorists' Target Selection," *Terrorism and Political Violence* 10, no. 2 (1998), 53–85.

assertion however, it should be noted that when looking into the lethality of the anti-federalist movement, as in many other analyses of terrorism, a question emerges as to how to treat a significant outlier. On the one hand, the inclusion of the outlier may negatively impact our understanding the nature of the phenomenon under investigation. On the other hand, the outlier is an inherent part of the phenomenon, despite its unique nature; thus, its exclusion may also be perceived as a distortion of the data. In the current analysis, results pertaining to casualties will be presented with and without the inclusion of the 1995 attack in Oklahoma.

To begin with, almost 15% of the Militias' attacks caused, or were intended to cause, mass casualties. This is the highest proportion among all components of the American far right. Second, the average number of fatalities and injuries is considerably higher than that found among the groups comprising the racist movement (14.04 injured and 3.97 fatalities); when omitting the attack in Oklahoma, the average goes down considerably (0.77 and 0.55 respectively). Nonetheless, the average is still higher than what we find in some of the other movements. Thus, it may be concluded that while the number of attacks produced by the Militias is still not necessarily on the rise, the destructive potential of their attacks is relatively high.

5.2.4 – Analyzing Violence of the Fundamentalist Block

As described in the first part of this study, the ongoing decline of the *Aryan Nations*, the most powerful Identity group in the 1980s and 1990s, culminated in 2004 with the death of its founder and idolized Pastor Richard Butler. Shortly thereafter, while officially still led by successor August Kries III, the organization began to lose cohesiveness. Some of the more well-known splinter groups of the AN were Alabama's *Aryan Nations-United Church of Yahweh*, which later entirely omitted the term *Aryan Nations* from the its name, led by Jonathan Williams and Clark Patterson, and Jay Faber's group, *Aryan Nations Revival*, based in New York. But probably the most successful of the AN's descendants is Paul Mullet's *Crusaders of Yahweh*, with branches in no less than 17 states. Just recently the organization was able to garner further publicity when Mullet filed paperwork to be a lobbyist on Capitol Hill, explaining that "[t]he white race is being targeted as a hate group. Everywhere we turn, we are being depicted as a bunch of inbreeds. ... It is time we take a stand..."[420]

Besides the AN's splinter groups, the current influential Identity organizations include Pete Peter's *Scriptures for America/La Porte Church of Christ*, Dan Gayman's *Church of Israel*, and Chuck Kuhler's *Virginia Christian Israelites*. Assessments indicate that the overall movements include between 25,000 and 50,000 members and approximately 60–70 active ministers.[421]

The historical review of the Identity groups' operational development already indicated that in comparison to their counterparts on the far right scene, they were the least violent, or at least the least likely to engage in militant activities. And while in the 1980s groups such as *The Order* and *Covenant, the Sword and the Arm of the Lord* gave the impression that the movement might change course for a more militant path, since then it is difficult to identify clearly violent campaigns whose origin could be traced to the Identity movement. An empirical examination supports this perception, as only 66 attacks were clearly linked to Identity groups, the smallest number among all streams; a significant proportion of these were perpetrated by members of AN (around half), demonstrating that the dominant status of AN was not limited to the ideological/organizational arena.

Probably one of the more interesting trends of the Identity's violence is that, unlike the overall far-right universe, or the other movements within it, the number of their acts of violence declined during the last decade. They were more active in the 1990s than in the

---

[420] Lauren Victoria Burke, "White Nationalist Neo-Nazi Group Registers to Lobby on Capitol Hill," *Politic365*, (20 June 2012), http://politic365.com/2012/06/20/white-nationalist-neo-nazi-group-registers-to-lobby-on-capitol-hill/ (accessed 4 November 2012).

[421] One of the more interesting groups to emerge from within the Christian identity movement was *Phineas Priesthood*; while information regarding the nature of the group is limited, the best description is of a generally leaderless social framework based mainly around Spokane, Idaho. The group promulgates the notion that murdering people who disobey God's laws by performing abortions, consorting romantically with someone from different race, or being a homosexual, is justified. They rely on the biblical story of Phineas to invoke God's blessing for their violent actions. While in our dataset we were able to identify two attacks which were perpetrated or planned by members of the movement, other accounts argue that the group was involved in additional attacks on mixed-race couples and abortion facilities. Probably one of the reasons for confusion regarding the level of operation of the groups is that membership in the group is not exclusive; thus, members of *The Priesthood* were also apparently involved in the violent campaign of *The Order* as well as other Christian Identity and anti-abortionist groups. This is mainly because the process of joining the group requires only the decision to engage in *Priesthood* activities.

2000s: two-thirds of the attacks were perpetrated before 2001. So it seems that Identity-related violence did not merely erupt late, but also declined quicker than any other stream, and overall never reached the intensity of the other far right movements. To illustrate, only in one year—1994—did Identity groups produce a double-digit number of attacks.

In terms of geographical dispersion, two trends can be very carefully identified. The first is that half of the states never experienced attacks by Identity groups. Second, a significant proportion of Identity movement violence was perpetrated in what is known as the "White Bastion" of the Mid-Northwest: almost a quarter of the attacks were in Idaho, Washington State, and Iowa. This statistic is not completely surprising considering the location of the AN headquarters in Idaho and its influence in the region.

Operationally, Identity violence focuses on two types of targets: minorities and financial institutions. The first is easy to explain and is clearly related to the movement's ideological tenets. The latter is unusual, especially in comparison to the target selection of the other far right movements - albeit not completely surprising to find within the Identity realm, considering that both *The Order* and the *CSA* were involved in such practices. Most robberies were conducted by one group, the *Aryan Republican Army*, which was comprised mainly of former AN members and other Identity followers who were active mainly between 1994 and 1995, stockpiling ammunition and money, allegedly for funding and for implementing future operations. Other clear trends are the avoidance of attacks against property (6%) and relatively higher levels of mass-casualty attacks (13.6%), which are also related to the relatively high levels of lethality (0.34 fatalities and 2.49 injured per attack).

In contrast to the Identity movements, the anti-abortionists have been extremely productive during the last two decades, amassing 227 attacks, many of them perpetrated without the responsible perpetrators identified or caught. And while, in both cases, the 1990s were more violent than the last decade, in the case of anti-abortion, the trend is much more extreme, as 90% of attacks were perpetrated before 2001. Other differences are reflected in the geographical dispersion of anti-abortion violence, which exists across the country, with California and Florida experiencing the highest number of attacks. This includes an emphasis on damage to property rather than to human beings, as the great majority of the attacks (more than 70%) were intended to cause damage to abortion clinics rather than cause direct harm to people. For that reason, the average number of victims is also the lowest among all streams of the far right (0.03 fatalities, and 0.27 injured).

5.3 – Comparative Perspective and Unidentified Perpetrators

After reviewing the characteristics of the violence manifested by the different far right groups, the current section will emphasize a comparative perspective which will help to devise a hierarchy based on the level of threat posed by the different groups. In addition, it will examine the relatively large number of attacks in which the perpetrators where not identified, in order to understand if these share some similar traits, and how these are different from the attacks in which perpetrators were identified.

Historically, the academic and professional literature has been inconsistent in conceptualizing the terrorist threat. While some have evaluated the threat based on the number of attacks perpetrated by the terrorist groups, others have focused more on their durability and tangible assets. Some scholars, however, have preferred to ignore both and focus on the number of casualties produced by the attacks of the group, often discounting both the frequency of the group's attacks and its overall operational capabilities. Thus, for example, although Al-Qaeda's only successful attack on US soil was almost 12 years ago, it is still considered the most significant terrorist threat, mainly as a result of the magnitude of casualties its attacks produced, and its perceived tendency to continue to produce mass-casualty attacks.

In the current study several components have been included in order to estimate the relative threat posed by different groups, including the number of attacks and their proportion in recent years; the number of attacks, successful or attempted, which resulted in mass casualties; tactics; target selection; and average number of victims. The overall findings are presented in Table 4 and provide several important insights. The most important is the applicability of the iceberg model to describe American far right violence. As can be observed, the number of violent acts that are produced by unaffiliated individuals is extremely high; moreover, these attacks are usually unsophisticated—only 1% of the attacks included the use of firearms or explosives, well below what could be observed in any other group or stream. Thus, in most cases we are concerned with spontaneous beatings of minorities or vandalism of facilities. It is possible to assume that the perpetrators of these attacks are the future recruitment potential of the more institutionalized and formal violent streams. In other words, after crossing the line and performing minor attacks on their own initiative, at some point such individuals may seek more organized, systematic mechanisms to express their convictions, and thus will join more formal streams of the American far right. It also appears that the KKK, with its current informal and fragmented structure and low level of operational sophistication is the formal movement that is closest to the base of the iceberg, and may be the first station for those joining the conventional American far right.

Table 4 – Comparative evaluation of Far right violence

Group/movement	Number of attacks*	1990s vs. 2000s ratio	Proportion of mass casualty attacks	Proportion of attacks with Fire arms	Proportion of attacks with explosives	Proportion of attacks against human targets	Avg. number of injured	Avg. number of fatalities	Avg. number of casualties
KKK	264	0.123	3%	10.9%	7.1%	28.5%	0.39	0.07	0.46
Neo-Nazi	124	0.362	3.2%	31.4%	10.4%	83.1%	1.65	0.35	2.00
Skinheads	205	0.265	2.4%	21.4%	0.04%	96%	.73	0.24	0.97
Militias	87	1.23	14.9%	63.2%	67.8%	90.8%	14.04 / 0.77**	3.97 / 0.55**	18.01 / 1.32**
Christian Identity	66	1.64	13.6%	65.1%	19.6%	94%	2.49	0.34	2.83
Anti-Abortion	227	8.08	7%	10.1%	23.3%	26.2%	0.27	0.03	0.30
Unaffiliated	3354	0.09	1.8%	0.07%	0.05%	52.1%	0.49	0.08	0.57

* The lower the number, the more active the group is during the 2000s in comparison to its level of activity during the 1990s.
** Excluding the 1995 Oklahoma attack

Abiding by the same logic, the higher we climb to the top of the iceberg, the more lethal the group's attacks, and the smaller they are in the number of attacks. Thus, while the Christian Identity groups were involved in the least number of attacks, on average these have generated the highest number of victims (injured + fatalities). The Skinheads are ranked fourth in terms of number of attacks, and in terms of the likelihood of causing mortal harm. Lastly, the Militias and neo-Nazis are ranked second and third in terms of number of attacks and casualties—not taking the 1995 attack in Oklahoma into account. While the unaffiliated have a slightly higher level of lethality in comparison to the KKK and anti-abortionists, overall the iceberg model fits the findings, as there is a clear base which is wider in terms of the number of attacks, while the narrower parts of the iceberg are indeed sharper (more lethal).

However, lethality is not the entire story when seeking to evaluate current threats, as trends over time are no less important. As the findings in the 1990s/2000s ratio column illustrate, some groups have become much less active during the last decade, while others have intensified their violence. First, it is clear that the number of spontaneous unaffiliated attacks has been on the rise in the last decade, which is a source of concern if this is the future recruitment potential of the more established far right groups. Second, in general violence perpetrated by the anti-abortionists and, on a smaller scale, the Christian Identity and Militia groups, is in decline, at least in comparison to the last decade of the twentieth century. Combining the anti-abortionist focus in the last two decades on vandalism, and their relatively declining volume of violence, probably makes them a less salient threat. And while the Christian Identity groups and the Militias are more effective in their attacks, the discourse about their return or growing threat seems somewhat exaggerated. That leaves us with the Skinheads and the neo-Nazi groups, both of which were more active in the last decade than in the 1990s, as well as in the top ranks in terms of lethality. Maybe it is no coincidence that the most recent mass-casualty attack by far right elements in the United States was perpetrated by an individual affiliated with the HMS.[422]

---

[422] In the morning hours of 5 August, 2012, at around 10am, Wade Michael Page, a 40 year-old from Cudahy Wisconsin, arrived at a parking lot at Sikh temple in Oak Creek, Wisconsin and began firing at the temple's inhabitants using a Springfield XD(M) 9-millimeter automatic pistol which he had purchased several days earlier. He then entered the temple and continued killing parishioners until eventually he was shot by members of the local police force. He killed six worshipers and a police officer.

Other conclusions which can be extracted from the findings presented in Table 4 raise interesting questions. First, the two groups most involved in mass-casualty attacks—Christian Identity and Militias—are the most lethal. Nonetheless, overall the great majority of attacks are perpetrated against specific individuals or facilities, and the far right has limited tendencies or capabilities to engage in mass-casualty attacks. This may be the result of limited capabilities, an attempt to avoid further de-legitimization—important mainly for groups operating in the domestic arena—or because they are not deprived groups which feel hopeless. The latter assumption is compatible with some of the more popular explanations for extreme violence, such as suicide terrorism. For instance, Pape emphasized that groups who adopt this tactic are mostly those whose constituency is suffering long-term occupation.[423]

The Militias and the Christian Identity groups are also more prominent in terms of their use of firearms and explosives. Whereas this is understandable in the case of the Militias as they are striving to employ paramilitary characteristics, it is not initially clear why this is the case with the Identity groups. Two explanations may be suggested. First, as posited by some scholars, the stronger the group's agenda is framed in religious and totalistic ideas, the more it will be willing or determined to use exceptionally lethal tactics. The growing literature on the new terrorism is particularly supportive of the notion that the last three decades have witnessed not just the rise of religious terrorism, but of more spectacular tactics which aim to maximize the number of casualties, and that these two trends are causally linked.[424] The second explanation may stem from the isolated nature of many of the Identity groups. While the Skinheads and the KKK members are in many cases a part of the social fabric of a specific community, this is not the case with many members of Identity groups. Thus, this isolation, which creates a social distance between the members of the group and mainstream society, may serve not just as a foundation for radicalization, but may facilitate a stronger sense of alienation towards the mainstream culture and willingness to engage in harmful activities.

---

[423] Robert Pape, "The Strategic Logic of Suicide Terrorism," American Political Science Review, 97(3) (2003), 1–19.

[424] Laqueur; Ian O. Lesser, et al., Countering the New Terrorism (Santa Monica: The Rand Corporation, 1999). On the subject of religious terrorism, see Juergensmeyer.

Finally, it is possible to identify a clear separation between the groups that are human-target oriented, and groups that are vandalism-oriented. The neo-Nazi, Skinhead, Militias and Christian Identity groups fall into the category of groups which direct their violence against human targets, which constitute at least three-quarters of their attacks; the KKK, anti-abortionists and unaffiliated groups comprise the second category, as attacks against property constitute around half of their attacks. Overall, this further supports the conclusions of the threat analysis provided earlier in this section.

6. Concluding Remarks

The current study has striven to provide academics and practitioners with a better understanding of the past and current landscape of the violent American far right. The compilation and analysis of a comprehensive dataset of far right violence and complementary ideological typology allowed for the identification of systematic structural and behavioral trends, as well as the investigation of related theoretical and conceptual questions.

While many still tend to ignore the fact that the American far right is an accumulation of different actors, and place most of its components in the same analytical category, the current study has illustrated that these different components are not merely driven by competing ideological tenets, but are also significantly idiosyncratic in the ways they manifest their ideology in the operational, often violent, realm. This illustrates that ideology and behavior are linked and nurture each other in the organizational frameworks of the American violent far right. From a theoretical perspective, this constitutes a further indication of the perception among some parts of the academic community that terrorism is an instrument of symbolic discourse which is shared by violent groups and their adversaries. Target selection is thus not based just on operational considerations, but is one component, among others, which allows violent groups to shape their message using violent practices—timing, weapons used and target locations, are only a small measure of the other components which contribute to the shape of the symbolic message conveyed via the attack. In this context, policy implications are clear. If the numerous far right groups are driven by different ideological sentiments, and are thus also engaged in distinguishing tactics, then the response in terms of counterterrorism policies must be flexible and group/movement oriented. Particularly relevant in this sense are the findings presented in chapter 5, which provide a roadmap regarding target selection and tactics which have characterized each of the far right movements.

This study also sought to explain how both exogenous and endogenous factors may shape the characteristics of American far right violence, including political, demographic and economic factors. For example, a contentious political climate and ideological political empowerment play important roles in increasing the volume of violence; thus, it is not only feelings of deprivation which motivate those involved in far right violence, but also the sense of empowerment which emerges when the political system is perceived to be increasingly open to far right ideas. And while the theoretical implications of these findings have already been discussed in length in chapter 4, it is worth mentioning that these trends contradict predominant perceptions in the field which associate motivational forces that facilitate political violence with the unbalanced allocation of goods, and provide support for explanations which focus on correlations between violence and perceived changes in the sociopolitical structure.

While the findings are not particularly strong with regard to the relationship between the level of violence and the economic factors, when looking at the trends in violence not only in relation to the time vector, but also across space, and considering demographic indicators, it is clear that the violence is concentrated in heterogeneous areas, thus supporting theoretical assumptions associating intra-community violence with community cohesiveness and its members' perceptions regarding the collective's boundaries. It is therefore clear from a policy perspective that more effort is needed to create effective integration mechanisms in areas in which we see growing ethnic, religious and cultural diversity.

Besides the above, the study includes numerous additional insights which raise new questions for further research, such as the perceived limited correlation between the level of violence and the proportion and size of certain minority groups, i.e., Hispanic groups; changing trends in cooperation between various ideological streams; the shift of the violence from the South to other parts of the country; changes in the balance of power within the movements; and the clear decline of some of the groups, such as the anti-abortionists. These issues indicate that this study represents a point of departure for further exploration of the American far right, rather than strictly an additional source of knowledge.